BUTTERFLY
BRAIN

Also by Barry Cryer

You Won't Believe This, But
Pigs Can Fly

BARRY CRYER

BUTTERFLY BRAIN

Weidenfeld & Nicolson

LONDON

First published in Great Britain in 2009
by Weidenfeld & Nicolson

1 3 5 7 9 10 8 6 4 2

A CIP catalogue record for this book
is available from the British Library.

ISBN- 97 8 02978 5910 9

Typeset by Input Data Services Ltd,
Bridgwater, Somerset

Printed and bound in the UK by
CPI Mackays, Chatham ME5 8TD

Weidenfeld & Nicolson

The Orion Publishing Group Ltd
Orion House
5 Upper Saint Martin's Lane
London, WC2H 9EA

The Orion Publishing Group's policy is to use papers that
are natural, renewable and recyclable products and made
from wood grown in sustainable forests. The logging
and manufacturing processes are expected to conform to
the environmental regulations of the country of origin.

www.orionbooks.co.uk

The Preamble [1]

It was the best of times, it was the worst of times ...

The opening line of a book is all-important, so what better mentor than Charles Dickens?[2] I wish to engage your attention, dear reader, but panic not. I am not about to embark on *Oliver Twist* or *Great Expectations* but rather a collection of anecdotes, attributions, allusions, appraisals and other words beginning with 'a'.[3] More to the point, memories of times past and people met.

My late writing partner, Ray Cameron, once said, 'I wish I could just once say something that didn't remind you of something else.' 'Funny you should say that,' I said, 'that reminds me ...'

Unfortunately, this habit of making endless connections is incurable, hence our title, so forgive me if I flit about

---

1 The prelude to a ramble.

2 The actor Emlyn Williams, whose one-man performances of *Bleak House* became legendary, told me he was once asked to do a 'turn' (see 2a below) at a charity evening in London. He was at a loss, and then hit on the idea of a Dickens reading lasting around ten minutes. It went well and afterwards a producer approached him. The producer thought there was a whole show in the idea. Emlyn told me that it soon took over his life. He even had a shared joke with the audience where he would turn the page over every few moments to give the illusion that he was reading. Everyone knew he had memorised every word of every line. He toured the world for more than thirty years as Dickens. He said, 'Some people have forgotten I'm an actor.' Nobody who saw the show would ever have thought that. 2a For younger readers – yes you, Wayne – a 'turn' was an act, what is now known to young stand-ups as a 'set'.

3 See *Roget's Thesaurus of English Words and Phrases*. Revised edition (1990).

during the course of this book. Just hang on to your hats and keep your eye on the footnotes, because the butterfly is about to take off.

I am seventy-four as I write this and I may be older by the time I finish it.[4]

Anythin' for a quiet life, as the man said when he took the situation at the lighthouse.

Charles Dickens again, this time Sam Weller in *The Pickwick Papers*. Although I've never wanted anything approaching a quiet life.

> Out, out, brief candle!
> Life's but a walking shadow, a poor player
> That struts and frets his hour upon the stage
> And then is heard no more: it is a tale
> Told by an idiot, full of sound and fury,
> Signifying nothing.

That's more like it. Bill Shakespeare,[5] of course, whose plays are stuffed with quotations.[6] He's not the only one:

Brief and powerless is man's life; on him and all his race the slow, sure doom falls pitiless and dark.

BERTRAND RUSSELL[7]

---

4 If you're reading this in paperback, I'm seventy-five.
5 *Macbeth*, Act 5, Scene 5. In which Soames visits his wife Irene.
6 'Now we sit through Shakespeare in order to recognize the quotations.' – Orson Welles.
7 A taxi driver once told me he had Bertrand Russell in the back of his cab. He was 'a bit of a clever dick', quoth the cabbie, a pithy but not wholly inaccurate definition, I think you'll agree.

But enough of flippancy. Bert (I use the familiar, even though I never met him) also said:

> Man is not a solitary animal, and so long as social life survives self-realisation cannot be the supreme principle of ethics.[8]

To wit, 'no man is an island', as John Donne averred. Although I'm prone to mention that they named Barry Island after me. But seriously,[9] a life lived in isolation with only four walls for company, or even a pavement, is too tragic to contemplate. I thank God that I have rarely experienced it. Loneliness is an endemic plague that affects so many people. I try to remember, each and every morning, that I have a wonderful wife, four children, seven grandchildren (at the last count) and many friends. I think, how fortunate I am.[10] Alright, alright, 'you're lucky, Cryer, tell us about some *hard* luck.' Well, I've had quite a few operations, but who hasn't? Many rejections, both in a personal and professional capacity, and ... err ... enough! The Bard, again:

> As good luck would have it.[11]

So, as the butterfly flaps its wings once again, I leave you

---

8 Please note that for the remainder of this book, I'll be quoting from *Butterfly Brain* by Barry Cryer, Orion Books (2009).
9 As if what had gone before had you holding your side, groaning 'enough, enough'.
10 Sounds of muffled yawns.
11 *The Merry Wives of Windsor*, Act 3, Scene 5. In which Soames confronts Young Jolyon and Irene at Robin Hill. It's hotting up!

in the capable hands of the songbird laureate, Gracie Fields:

Wish me luck as you wave me goodbye.[12]

---

12 Words by Phil Park.

The Ramble

I have always been delighted at the prospect of a new day, a
fresh try, one more start, with perhaps a bit of magic waiting
somewhere behind the morning.

J.B. PRIESTLEY

Key facts
Proudest moment: Heckling His Holiness the Pope in St Peter's
Square. 'Where's your missus?' I shouted. What japes!
Unhappiest moment: Being arrested by the Vatican guard.
Ambition: To win the Job Centre lifetime achievement award.

I had a phone call a while back about a celebration for Roy
Hudd's fifty years in show business. The man asked me how
long I'd been in the business. 'If you're talking about my first
paid job, then it's fifty-three years.'[1]
 Fifty-three years since that day in 1956, when I was offered
a week at the Leeds City Varieties Theatre.[2] I've said it before,
and I'll say it again:[3] I've been dogged by good luck. I never
planned my career. A year after I appeared at the City Varieties I took a train to London on a seventeen-day ticket and

---

[1] When Mozart was my age he had written 42 symphonies, 27 concertos and 16
operas. And had been dead for over 40 years.
[2] Five days of walking on and offstage to the sound of my own feet.
[3] And again on pp.256, 457 and 801.

on the sixteenth day I got a job as a bottom-of-the-bill comic at the Windmill Theatre.[4] From there, I began writing revues for Danny La Rue and even released a record that went to number one in Finland.[5] Then, in the early 1960s I met David Frost, who invited me to join the writing roster on not only 'The Frost Report' but also many of his other shows. In the 1970s and 1980s, I was fortunate enough to team up with a series of wonderful writers and work with Morecambe and Wise, Tommy Cooper, Kenny Everett, Les Dawson and many others. The 1970s also brought 'I'm Sorry I Haven't A Clue' into my life and for that, I'll be eternally grateful. Then, in the 1990s, I went back to performing and touring; first with Willie Rushton, and now with Colin Sell and Ronnie Golden. I still do the odd bit on radio and TV and retirement is a four-letter word.[6] You don't retire in this business: the phone just stops ringing.

I can honestly say that this is the best time of my life. I haven't had a career, more a series of incidents. The only vague plan I had was to make a living at the thing I loved, to marry and have children. And that was it. It may surprise you to learn that I don't consider myself to be a comedian. I just sing songs and tell jokes. I'm an entertainer and an archivist – I've got a good memory.[7] I never wanted to be a star because I never felt I had the 'X Factor' needed to become one. I think the really good ones – Spike Milligan, Tony

---

4 When I was working at the Windmill, I got to know a man called Bruce Forsyth. I wonder what happened to him.
5 This may have had something to do with the fact that they gave away a car with each record.
6 In a kind of ten-letter way.
7 It's a good job too, because we have a long meander ahead.

Hancock, Peter Cook, and the rest – had an air of self-destructive madness about them which I've never personally felt. I don't have the introspective nature needed to reach that level. I've had my lows, I've made my bad decisions and sometimes I've frightened myself, but I've had a go and, by and large, it's worked out.

In short, I've been lucky enough to be in the right place at the right time on so many occasions. I've wandered through doors that have led to the most wonderful experiences as a writer, and not for a minute have I had what you might call a 'career plan'. I've gone with the flow and somehow it's all turned out very well. Earlier, I mentioned Emlyn Williams as an example of how this kind of chance happening or meeting can sometimes transform your life. There have been rejections and disappointments, naturally, but more often than not things seem to have worked out for me. I can honestly say that all of it has involved very little planning. In life in general, I try not to analyse things too much, because I like to think that every day is a new one. I get up in the morning with the attitude that when it's over, I'll go back to bed looking forward to the next day. It's a simple philosophy, but it's stood me in good stead and brought me many happy memories.

Willie Rushton once told me that I'd drop dead in the middle of a gag. I can see his point, but I hope it doesn't happen, or at least not yet, because there's still plenty I'd like to do.[8]

---

8 About 200 pages, for a start.

By the Way, This is not an Autobiography [1]

Autobiography is an unrivalled vehicle for telling the truth
about other people.

PHILIP GUEDALLA [2]

You won't believe this, but my first book [3] was meant to be
an autobiography. When it was finished, my agent phoned
me up and said, 'Barry, where are *you* in all this?' My aforementioned penchant for anecdotes had meant that I'd forgotten to include anything about me. A novice's mistake in
writing an autobiography, but I came by it honestly.

The truth is that I hardly ever look inwards and I'm not really
one for self-reflection or too much analysis. I much prefer the
company of other people to my own. I think this need for
sociability probably comes from the fact that my father died
when I was very young. [4] John Carl Cryer was a Masonic
golfing accountant, which is about as far away from a description of me as you can get. I have very vague memories of him,
but if I was listening to a recording of his voice right now,
I probably wouldn't recognise it. My mother never remarried

---

1 I hope you kept the receipt.
2 As you will recall, Guedalla was the editor of *Slings and Arrows: Sayings Chosen
from the Speeches of the Rt. Hon. David Lloyd George* (1929). I believe it's on everybody's
bookshelves.
3 *You won't believe this, but* by Barry Cryer, Virgin Books (1998).
4 Not that I'm analysing, you understand.

and she hardly ever spoke about him after his death.

So apart from a few photos and, several years ago, a chat with someone who knew him, I have nothing tangible to connect me to my dad. I wonder whether my relentless seeking out of other people – to swap ideas, to work and to socialise with, was an attempt to replace my dad.[5]

In many ways, these factors also mean that I had what you might call a classic 'gay upbringing'. After all, my father had died, my brother was away for long periods with the Merchant Navy and I was this young bloke with vague theatrical ambitions, alone at home with my mother. However, had I been gay, I don't think I would've been aware that there were any gay people living in Leeds at all. Maybe I was naïve or maybe this ignorance was understandable, given that the shameful intolerance of the time meant people had to hide their sexuality. It was different when I moved to London, of course, and met gay performers at the Windmill. Then I merely wondered what the big deal had been. That I then went on to work with people like Frankie Howerd, Kenny Everett[6] and Graham Chapman probably stemmed from this rather matter-of-fact empathy. This was generated in spite of, not because of, my rather conservative Leeds upbringing.

---

5 The comedian and actor Robin Williams said that he once shouted at his son when he was five years old, 'Behave, behave! You were out of order. You never do that again.' And then he said, 'Behind me was the ghost of my father saying "revenge".'

6 As Kenny Everett once said to me, 'Ooh Baa. Married for over 30 years. Four children. What a smokescreen!'

Yorkshire

Patriotism is your conviction that this country is superior to all others because you were born in it.

GEORGE BERNARD SHAW

My Yorkshire Credentials

23 March 1935	Barry Charles Cryer is born at 3 a.m. in an all-nite drive-thru maternity ward in Leeds.
7 September 1947	Enters Leeds Grammar School.
11 June 1952	Voted School Bully.
2 September 1955	Enters Leeds University. BA Eng. Lit. (Failed). He failed due to the outbreak of the Second World War, which was sixteen years before, but upset him very deeply.
18 April 1956	Offered a week at Leeds City Varieties Theatre. Five days of walking on- and offstage to the sound of my own feet.[1]

A Radio Leeds presenter rang me recently to do an interview, as I was about to do a show in the city. She asked me how long I'd been down south, and I told her it was now quite a

---

1 See page 5 for the first time that line was used.

bit longer than I'd lived up north. I left Leeds when I was twenty-one and now I'm seventy-four,[2] so in fact it's more than fifty years since I've lived there.

'I can tell,' she said. 'It's your accent.'

'Oh,' I said, a little taken aback. 'So what would you say my accent is now?'

'Radio 4 posh,' came the reply.

I was a tad hurt. My friends in the south know that I'm a Yorkshireman, because of what Alan Bennett calls 'the incurable disease of the vowels' that affects all northerners' nasal tones. I'd hoped my friends in the north would feel the same.

So if my voice *has* changed, am I still a Yorkshireman?

I love Yorkshire, and I'm very proud of the place but I'm also mindful of the George Bernard Shaw quoted from above. I can't see the logic of having pride in a place just because you were born there and I've always been wary of playing the professional Yorkshireman. It's an easy role to do and once you start it's hard to get out of. So I've never gone round saying, 'I'm a Yorkshireman, me.' If it comes up in conversation that's great; especially if the other person is from Leeds and remembers it how I do. Other than that, I don't think about it very much. However, there are times when it's thrust upon you. For instance, when I first went down to London and came back to Leeds a few months later, someone said to me, 'How are you liking it down there?' The implication was that I would be back pretty soon. This attitude also once found its way

---

2 Again, seventy-five if you're reading a paperback.

into a chat show I was doing, when the presenter said to me:

'Your Yorkshire accent has become more pronounced now the camera is rolling.'

'Yes, it's called Parkinson's Disease,' I said and immediately regretted it.

There was an intake of breath from the audience and they never actually used that bit. I was relieved because I didn't mean it badly, it was just that the host was trying to root out the closet southerner in me and my pride had been hurt. Unfortunately for me, this wasn't the only time that I'd be put on the spot in front of a Yorkshire audience. Many years ago I was on another chat show in Leeds with Barry Took.[3] The presenter was Austin Mitchell, now MP for Grimsby, and he said to me:

'You were born here, you must be proud of that.'

The audience murmured its approval.

'No, not really,' I replied. 'It's just a matter of fate that my mother happened to be here at the time.'

Blame George Bernard Shaw. However, I am happy to say that when I play Leeds these days, I do notice that I get a good reception. Perhaps they're thinking, 'He's one of us. He might live down south, but nobody's perfect.'

The more we elaborate our means of communication, the less we communicate.

JOSEPH PRIESTLEY[4]

---

3 How could they tell the difference?
4 I don't think he's related to J. B. but you can tell he's a Yorkshireman nonetheless.

I might be a fan of the American style of one-liners, but I'm
also a sucker for that dour, lugubrious humour from the
north of England, especially the sort that comes with a
hidden twinkle. It's so characteristic of Yorkshire; humour
that is misunderstood at the start but then comes good at
the punch line. I'm reminded of a story that Joe Brown[5] once
told me. He had played a gig in Leeds and he went for a pint
in the local before the show. He was recognised by two older
men and they soon started talking about the Second World
War and their experiences of it. One of them said:

'Joe, during the war do you know that I marched across
Yugoslavia from one end to the other, and when I got to the
end, my boots . . .'

'Boots?' said his companion.

It's like one of my favourite cartoons, which shows an
old man in a pub and a young couple sitting opposite
him. He's saying, 'Local character, fund of anecdotes, buy
me a pint and I'll piss off.' The desire not to get too big
for your boots, whether you've walked across Yugoslavia in
them or not, is redolent of Yorkshire. This is a little island
and Yorkshire is quite a large slab of it. It's a bit like the
Texas of England and, like the US state, it comes with the
same strange mixture of being full of itself but not wanting
anyone to know it. I tend to like people who are arrogant

---

5 Joe Brown is a great example of someone who, although notorious for his sharp
tongue, knew how to be economical with his wit. He was once a guest on the famous
Simon Dee show in the Sixties and was coming under fire from Simon's usual barrage
of barbs. They culminated in Simon asking Joe if he'd like to play his 'dreadful new
single'. Joe once told me that ten responses flashed through his mind before he
settled on 'Alright then'. Suddenly, he was the victim and the audience was completely
on his side. As a response, it probably worked better than any of those comebacks
he could've offered.

in their humility and perhaps this is where it comes from. That spiritual northerner, David Nobbs, tells a story about two girls he overheard on a bus outside Harrogate. One of them was relating her experiences of a film premiere she'd seen in London, where she'd been behind the red rope with all the autograph hunters and well-wishers.

'Brad Pitt come along the red carpet, as close to me as you are now.'

'Brad Pitt!' said the other girl, her face lighting up. 'What was he like?'

'He wouldn't be much at a bus stop,' her friend replied.

With this in mind, it surprises me that compared to Lancashire, the number of comedians Yorkshire has produced seems to be minimal. Ernie Wise, Frankie Howerd and Charlie Williams are the ones I can name off the top of my head, but it's a small list when you look across the Pennines and see how many that have come from Lancashire, especially Liverpool. Maybe that's because humour in the north-west is geared towards an 'end-of-the-pier' sensibility and consequently has travelled better. After all, there's no shortage of Yorkshire writers – Alan Bennett, Ted Hughes, Keith Waterhouse, J.B. Priestley, Andrew Marvell and the Brontë sisters, to name but several, but why Yorkshire humour travels better in print is a mystery to me.

I think television has seen off the north–south divide in terms of humour. Peter Kay is one of the biggest stars we have in comedy, and he can sell out weeks in London with no problems. On the face of it, Peter might seem a very northern comedian, after all, *Phoenix Nights* is about as parochial as you get, but the cleverness of his humour comes from simply being traditional. His world is families, weddings, funerals and old aunties. That stuff travels far. It could be old-fashioned, but when you're as good as Peter is, it feels very fresh. He's also very physical, constantly moving around the stage and using gesture to get his point across. That visual element makes his stuff accessible.

There used to be a fear among English comedians of crossing the border into Scotland. Max Miller's agent once got him a booking in Glasgow. Max refused to go, saying he was 'a comedian, not a missionary'. Conversely, Scots comedians didn't really travel south until Billy Connolly and Chic Murray[6] broke the mould.

---

6 Although a hugely popular comedian in his day, I think Chic is sadly overlooked now.

Loiners & Leodensians

I grew up in Harehills, in east Leeds. My wife Terry, who is from Brighton, pronounces it 'Hare Hills' but I still struggle to say it any other way than 'Air Ills'. I still flatten the 'a', as in bath and grass, and if I wish someone luck, it's always of the 'gud' variety. It's why I enjoy listening to Jimmy Savile if he's on the telly. Not only does he retain the accent, I'm sure it's become stronger as time's passed. I did a charity walk around the cricket pitch at Headingly a few years ago and Jim was there, sporting the usual fetching gold lamé tracksuit and chuffing on a fat cigar.

'You're a shy little violet, aren't you, Jim?' I said.

'Barrington, Barrington,' he replied. 'They do not ask me here to be unobtrusive. I am here to show off and make some noise.'

He was right, and he's adored for it, especially among the many kids who were there that day. He never talked down to them and treated them just as he would treat anyone else. Terry and I once took part in a 'Jim'll Fix It' by performing a miniature version of the 'Good Old Days' show for a 104-year-old woman in a nursing home. When she fell asleep during a break in the filming, Jim said:

'I think we should get on with it, it'll be toes-up time any moment.'

He was warm and solicitous to her, but he also had the

classic Yorkshire thing of not being too mawkish or sentimental.

Tony Harrison, the poet and playwright, retains his Leeds accent and has used it to brilliant effect in some of his work. He was a contemporary of mine both at Leeds Grammar School and the city's university and I remember him as a wonderfully dour character who didn't want to conform. However, he did show an interest in our shows at the university but was horrified at the thought of having to wear evening dress on stage. So the rest of the cast, including me, attacked him in the dressing room, forced the penguin suit on him and spread Brylcreem all over his wild hair. We soon tamed it into a smoothly parted affair and re-named him 'Lord Sleekhead of Gloss'. We made sure we'd get him on-stage and he good-naturedly agreed to do so.[1]

I also spent time in Leeds doing the 'Good Old Days' show, which ran for thirty years and was filmed live at the City Varieties. I often did it with Bernard Cribbins in a kind of double act. The chairman was Leonard Sachs who made that role famous with the long words and convoluted turns of phrase. The show wasn't entirely faithful to the original days of music hall, because in those times the chairman was a pub landlord and the whole thing was probably a lot more

---

1 A few months ago I listened to Radio 4's 'Front Row' programme because Tony was on it. Mark Lawson, the presenter, said, 'You were at university with Barry Cryer, weren't you?' and Tony replied that he could remember a poem I'd contributed for the university magazine, which he edited. I'd forgotten all about it. It went like this:

Lot became naturally rather peeved
When his sex life came to a halt
Well wouldn't you, when you had to make do
With occasional pinches of salt?

knockabout, but it was a good representation and Leonard brought real style and elegance to his role. So many people wanted to be in the audience, dressed in Edwardian finery, that the waiting list was twenty years long. It's hard to explain to younger people now how such an anachronism of a show was so popular, but it had huge TV audiences and the fact that it ran for thirty years speaks for itself.

Nostalgia doesn't come naturally to me, but I do still get the occasional attack. A few years ago, David Nobbs and I did an 'Audience With …' show at the National Media Museum in Bradford. Afterwards, a young couple came up to speak to me and rather enigmatically, the man said '12, Mount Pleasant Avenue. We live there.' We chatted away for a bit and it was nice to hear about who was living in the house where I grew up. I thought no more of it until last year, when I went up to Leeds again with our son Dave, who's doing the family tree. We went to Whitwell, just outside Leeds, where my dad grew up, and then on to the former family home in the aforementioned 'Air Ills'. Dave said, 'Well, we're here now, you might as well ring the door-bell.' A man answered and he said, 'We meet again.' For a moment, I was confused and then I recognised him. He invited us in, and it was one of those weird experiences where everything sort of looks the same, but doesn't at all. The décor was very drab in our day – all browns and dark oranges, but now the rooms were much brighter and lighter.

As we were about to leave, the man said to me, 'You didn't leave a ghost here, did you? My partner won't sit on the end of the sofa, because it's too cold.' I went over to the sofa. I sat down and immediately noticed it. 'Is it a draught from the outside?' I said. 'No,' he said, 'we've had everything checked and there are no gaps. It's weird.'

Speaking of ghosts, ITV announced in March this year that, as part of fierce budget cuts, the YTV studios on Kirkstall Road in Leeds would be shut down with the loss of many jobs. That was very sad news for everyone involved up there, and I felt it personally because I remember those studios opening at the end of the 1960s. 'Jokers Wild' was born in those Leeds studios and as the years went on I worked with both Les Dawson[2] and Frankie Howerd on programmes up there, among many others. It seemed a big leap in those days, making television programmes outside of London, but many people soon embraced it. It was noticeable that a lot of people, particularly technicians and camera crew, left London and never came back, having found property at very reasonable prices in the Dales. I went there recently to film the last 'Countdown' at the studios. I've done 'Countdown' many times, but since Richard Whiteley died and Carol Vorderman left, it's gone through various presenters and changes in its slot, and it's not quite the same show that it was. It'll be interesting to see how it fares after the move to Manchester.

About a year ago, I was in Dudley to do a Lifeboat Asso-

---

2 Although the 'tears of a clown' cliché can often be true, it was not the case with Les Dawson. What you saw onstage was exactly what you got offstage. Recently, I took part in a 'talking heads' style programme about Les where I went over all my old stories about him (see pp. 343, 478–490 & 803). However, the interviewer kept asking me to reveal Les's 'dark side'. I could see the camera crew pulling pained expressions of sympathy in my direction. Finally, she asked, 'Was there a Les Dawson that no one ever saw?' 'If there was a Les Dawson no one ever saw,' I replied 'no one ever saw him.'

ciation gig at the Town Hall[3] after I'd just finished recording 'Countdown'[4] with Des O'Connor. He'd recently taken over from Des Lynam as chairman. As is the usual format, we recorded five shows in one day and I'd been driven from Leeds to Dudley the following morning. I was just enjoying a steak sandwich and a beer in the restaurant of my hotel when this chap came over.

'Hello, Barry,' he said, 'my name's Dave, I'm a plasterer. My dad's dead.'

Now, that was some opening line, but I tried not to look fazed and I said that I was sorry to hear it.

'Oh, he loved you,' said Dave. 'Would you give him your autograph?'

I was slightly taken aback.

'I'm going to frame it,' was his rather puzzling explanation.

So I got a piece of paper from the bar, asked him his father's name, and dedicated it to the deceased man.

'I've seen you on "Countdown",' Dave remarked as I signed the paper.

'Funny you should say that,' I replied, 'I was only doing it yesterday.'

'Sorry,' said Dave, 'I missed it yesterday.'

'No no,' I said, 'we do them all in a day. We were with Des O'Connor.'

'Nah,' said Dave, shaking his head, 'I think you'll find it's Des Lynam. I saw him on Monday.'

---

3 This is relevant, I promise.
4 I told you.

I tried to explain that Des Lynam had *recorded* all his shows and had since left.

'We're now recording shows with Des O'Connor that will go out in January the following year.'

'Right,' said Dave uncertainly. 'Barry . . .?' He paused.

'Yes, Dave?' I prompted.

'When you're on it with Des O'Connor, could you do me a favour? Mention my dad. He'd have loved that.'

It had become one of those tangled conversations where I had to go over the whole story again. He eventually left and thanked me for the autograph. I was not entirely convinced that he thought I wouldn't suddenly pop up on 'Countdown' the following day and mention his dad.

On a personal note regarding the studios, when I consider that I'd been there at the beginning of that great Yorkshire institution, it did feel rather odd going back to those studios so near to their closure. Yet, despite having no regrets about moving south in those intervening years, here I am still flattening my vowels.

London

I hate quotations.[1]

As I may have mentioned earlier,[2] I came down to London from Leeds on a seventeen-day ticket and passed an audition the day before it ran out. My new job was as a bottom-of-the-bill comic at the Windmill Theatre in Soho and I often found myself listening to the sound of my own voice. The patrons had only come to see the strippers. In fact, the Windmill's boast during the Second World War had been 'we never closed', but the wags soon amended it to 'we never clothed'. Mind you, it was all tastefully done, fans, feather boas, and all, and the girls had to stand stock still while they posed. We used to hide behind the scenery and mutter jokes in their direction to see if they would wobble. Eventually, I left the Windmill and, after a stint in a show called *Expresso Bongo*,[3] began working in Winston's nightclub off Bond Street, initially just writing lines for Danny La Rue. Then a singer called Johnny Webb had a run-in with the management over something and walked out. I got a call from

---

1 Ralph Waldo Emerson (1803–1882).
2 Get used to it, folks!
3 A marvellous actor called Meier Tzelniker was also in *Expresso Bongo*. Some years later, we met on a train and chatted away. We got off at the same station and as we parted on the pavement, he turned back to me and said, 'Whatever happened to that fellow Cryer.'

Jack Hanson, Danny's manager, asking me to do the show that evening. Although I'd written the show, I didn't know it by heart, so I went on with a script. Suddenly, I found myself performing in the show as well. It was an exciting place to be. By the late 1950s, Winston's had become the celebrity club of choice. However, as is often the case with celebrity, a number of 'faces'[4] had begun to exert their influence on the club as well. When Danny told us he was leaving to fulfil a lifelong dream of running his own place, those of us who worked for him were more than a little concerned. We weren't sure how the club's management would react. As it happened, on the very night we planned to have a leaving party, a huge fight broke out between two rival gangs. I can't remember exactly how it started, save to say that when it did it was like something from a Western; tables, chairs and bottles flying everywhere. Rather than wait around for things to subside, we all made a discreet exit through the car park. It was a memorable end to a memorable stint.

With typical understatement, Danny named his new club in Hanover Square 'Danny La Rue's'. It soon became known simply as 'Danny's'. The guest list was typically understated too. As he'd done at Winston's, Danny managed to attract the likes of Richard Burton, Elizabeth Taylor, Judy Garland, Noël Coward and Princess Margaret[5] to the club. Despite the illustrious guest list, Danny's often looked soulless and tacky when it was empty, just like most nightclubs. However,

---

4 I remember one evening, being asked by Ronnie and Reggie Kray if I fancied a nightcap somewhere else. I was very much a civilian in that club and I wanted it to stay that way. In the best tabloid tradition, I thanked them, made my excuses and left.
5 I've got more if you want them.

it was transformed when the lights came on and Danny came out in one of his incredible outfits with the band in full cry. Danny was the first drag act to be a star, appearing in both the West End and on TV. He broke the mould of the traditional drag act, because he didn't play the role of a man pretending to be a woman. For a start, he hated the term female impersonator. He was simply a man who dressed up in women's clothing. I feel that, as a result, both the men and the women in the audience were able to relate to him. He would refer to his boobs and describe how he'd hang them up when it was hot. Then he'd stare at his crotch and exclaim 'Where does he put it?' before adding, 'I've been doing this for so long that when I whistle it goes away by itself.' Some of the other drag acts thought he was selling out but it obviously worked. His shows were hugely successful and at his height, he filled Blackpool Opera House every night for three months. He also had a show that ran at the Palace Theatre in London for two years. Danny really did break the mould.

My Friend, the Agent

It was during my time working for Danny that I met Roger Hancock, the brother of Tony and a show business agent. Although he was interested in representing me, he didn't want to take on a writer 'who's been up all night'. 'Carry on writing the shows for Danny, by all means,' he added, 'but if I'm going to represent you, I don't want you falling out of bed at midday with a head full of cotton wool.' Roger and I came to a gentleman's agreement. 'If I get pissed off with you, I walk away,' he said, 'and if you get pissed off with me, you do the same.' That was that. We didn't sign anything and forty years on, we're still together. Roger is virtually retired now and lives in Brighton, but we still speak regularly. I've yet to get pissed off.

His reputation in the business was as a driver of hard bargains. In fact, I'd sometimes sit in his Haymarket office while he negotiated a deal for me. He'd be on the phone saying things like 'Mr Cryer is a very busy man and what you're saying is ridiculous'. I'd be mouthing 'Take it! Take it!' but he'd give me a wink as he tied things up. Despite all the bluff and bluster, he was a very popular man and he never made enemies. He would come on very strong to someone and then go for a drink with them later on. He could shout at people, but he had warmth. They knew his heart was in the right place. The other agents knew that he was playing a game.[1] At first, he handled performers but he said that they drove him mad, so he switched to writer/performers like Graeme Garden, John Cleese and myself. As far as I'm concerned, it's always been a happy arrangement and I've never had a moment's trouble with the agency. To me it's like a good marriage; if it works don't fix it.

---

1 One of them, Michael Black, also a friend, had an office in the West End over a salt beef bar. His floor was so thin that if you stamped on it you could be heard below. He became friends with the people downstairs and they made up a code; one stamp was a cup of tea, two stamps a coffee, and three stamps a salt beef sandwich. He said that it worked very well until the day he auditioned a Flamenco dancer. He then told me the story of when the Inland Revenue wanted to see him. When they arrived, Michael said, 'Let's get down to basics. How much are we talking about?' The man mentioned a large sum of money. So Michael pulled a great wad from the drawer and asked the man if he took cash. He said, 'Not usually, Mr Black, but in this case, I will. Do you want a receipt?' Michael said, 'A receipt for cash? Are you mad?'

A Short Foulmouthed Tirade About Swearing

There ought to be a room in every house to swear in.

MARK TWAIN

It might be interesting for younger readers[1] to note that no swearing was allowed in the material we wrote for Danny. Personally, I have no problem with profanity as such, if used sparingly and well placed, but it takes style. I once asked Billy Connolly, the patron saint of the well-chosen expletive, why he swore so much and he said that it was part of his 'street rhythm', which is a fair point. However, Frank Skinner, a similarly brilliant exponent of the cuss, decided to leave out all of the swearing in his act one night and said it went just as well. Although he couldn't help restoring some the following night because he missed the sheer enjoyment of it. Don't forget, we're talking about Billy Connolly and Frank Skinner here. Lesser lights should beware of using an excess of expletives just for the sake of them. It often ruins a good set. I have a theory that if young stand-ups do swear more than their predecessors, it's because they have come through a tougher school of heckling audiences. They feel that they have to fight back in some way. Then, when they progress and

---

1 Don't fall asleep at the back, Wayne.

begin to face kinder audiences, it becomes difficult to change this now ingrained approach.[2]

Conversely, I don't like it when performers of my generation talk about young people as if all they do is swear and wear dirty jeans.[3] My generation forgets how much we were castigated once upon a time, and we should therefore make allowances. I think older performers should get out more and actually see a few younger comics in action. They would find that the scene out there is funny, refreshing and challenging. Personally, I don't really see a generation gap and prefer to be inspired by the younger generation. I'm enjoying life now as much as I've ever done, playing gigs, singing songs and creating new material. A few months ago, I met up in London with the actress and impressionist, Jan Ravens. Her twenty-year-old son, Arthur, who's just beginning a career as a stand-up, accompanied her. I was interested in him, he was interested in me, and we just talked and laughed for a couple of hours. He wasn't arrogant and neither was he over-deferential. It was a very happy evening. What generation gap?

All of which brings to mind that great old double act, Hubris and Nemesis.[4] When Gracie Fields made a farewell appearance at the end of her career at 'The Palladium of the North' (Batley Variety Club in Yorkshire), she threw a party for all the professionals in the area. Among them was a young comedian[5] who was on the up. He'd been to America, signed

---

2 End of lecture – next week I'll be discussing the joke as a cultural avatar de nos jours. Do join me.
3 At the same time? Call the police!
4 I wrote for them back in the 1970s.
5 Names have been withheld to protect the guilty.

a recording contract, and appeared several times at 'The Palladium of the South' (the Palladium). He was circulating the throng, talking of his exploits, when he was beckoned over by the lady herself. 'You can stay,' she said, 'but can the shit go?' Pungent, but I'm sure delivered with a twinkle. I've known contemporaries, struck by fame, who've disappeared into the odd world of celebrity. There is a true apocryphal story of the comedian who toiled for years in the clubs and small venues before getting a big break. He was catapulted by this good fortune into a rapid show business ascent, complete with a recording contract, top-of-the-bill appearances and a TV series. He became rather taken with it all and when his friends ceased to hear from him, he was crossed off everyone's Christmas card list. He got his comeuppance after some less-than-successful TV appearances and had the recording contract cancelled. He began ringing around his old friends, apologising and swearing that he would not succumb to such vanity again. They forgave him and he was welcomed back into the fold. However, within a year, fate smiled on him again and he was back on planet celebrity. This time he rang all the same friends and said, 'I'm a shit again.'

Anyway, back to the fucking swearing. When we were at Danny's, as was the case for everyone in those days, comics just didn't swear onstage at all. Instead, we were forced to be creative with our innuendo. For example, Danny and I created a character called Lady Cynthia Grope, a Conservative party stalwart, complete with twinset, pearls and blonde wig that eerily anticipated Margaret Thatcher. One of the cast would interview Lady Cynthia and she would deliver a torrent of double entendres in response. The key to it was that Danny played his lines innocently and merely let the audience do the work. Something that Humphrey Lyttelton[6] became a master at. I like to think that he would've approved of our use of what Humph used to call 'blue chip filth'. Although, as I was to famously discover, it was not to everyone's taste. One night, somebody stopped me in my tracks as I opened the show.

'This is satire, I suppose?' said a voice.

The voice seemed to be coming from a table containing Peter Sellers and Lionel Bart.[7] As neither had a gift for ventriloquism, I felt safe to answer back.

'No, it's nightclub filth. You need to get out more.'

I was told later that the voice belonged to John Lennon. It was not uncommon for members of The Beatles to turn up separately at Danny's. Years later, when I was working on one of David Frost's shows, Lennon turned up at the studio. He was with Yoko Ono by then and had become much less of an acerbic presence. Somehow, the two of us ended up in the Green Room, alone. He peered at me through his round glasses and said, 'Where do I know you from?' He paused. 'Danny's club?' I ventured. 'Was I a pig that night?' he said. I demurred. He concluded by saying 'I was out of it in those days, I don't remember much about them.' Ironically, I don't

---

6 Humph was never known to swear – not in my presence, anyway. However, I will never forget the last show he did with the *I'm Sorry I Haven't A Clue* company on our stage tour. We had a great night at the Harrogate Conference Centre and the next morning we were all gathered around the breakfast table at the hotel. Humph was sat in front of a bowl of prunes. He tasted the first one, grimaced and looked around the table. He said; 'How can you fuck up a prune?' Coming from anyone that's a funny line, but from him it was sublime.

7 I told you there was more.

remember much about the rest of the conversation, save to say that I told him I thought the beds at the Amsterdam Hilton Hotel were extremely comfy.[8]

---

8 This is a lie.

A Frosty Reception

Comedy, we may say, is society protecting itself – with a smile.

J.B. PRIESTLEY[1]

I had a number of lucky breaks early in my career, but by far the most significant was that night in the early 1960s that David Frost came into Danny's and, afterwards, asked who'd written the show. Before I knew it, the great mover and shaker had taken me under his wing. He asked me to write for a show called 'A Degree of Frost' and, once I'd passed the audition, I started work on 'The Frost Report'. I was officially a Frost writer, and a lot of doors began opening for you if you were one of those. I eventually had to tell Danny that I was leaving the club. When fellow Frost evacuee Ronnie Corbett also handed in his notice around the same time, Danny quipped, 'They'll be back.' I carried on writing for Danny, but it was my last time treading the boards in the nightclubs. Danny's was one of the last real cabaret nightclubs in London to host proper shows and I consider myself very lucky to have worked there, and for him.

After Danny, working with Frosty during the Sixties was no less frenetic.[2] I was lucky enough to be at the pilot of

---

1 I do read other authors but Priestley happens to be a favourite of mine.

'That Was The Week That Was', which David co-hosted with Brian Redhead, and it was an incredible two and a quarter hours long.[3] My wife Terry was with me that night, and I noticed her watching Brian and David intently. There you had the old pro and the younger pretender. Terry has an amazing ability to spot potential in people, and she turned to me and said, 'Watch out for that one.' What was most noticeable, apart from his delicate quiff, was that he was the one obviously running things. Most of Frosty's success comes from this entrepreneurial spirit and the fact that he's a great bringer together of people. I call him 'a practising catalyst'. He's also noted for his incredible memory and attention to detail. I've had the same phone number for over forty years now and whenever I see him, he always opens the conversation by reciting it. Writers liked Frosty because he would always talk to us and encourage us. He had a very clever way of rejecting a script. 'Not up to your usual standard,' he'd say, and you'd go back to work on it with renewed vigour. It was a great training ground. After all, the group of young writer-performers that went on to become Monty Python cut their teeth on 'The Frost Report'. Who can forget John Cleese in the now famous 'Class' sketch written by John Law, with Ronnie Corbett and Ronnie Barker?

---

2 I was at an awards ceremony at the Palladium. David Frost was the host and MC and I was one of the writers and warm-up men. I was standing with David and Eric Morecambe, and Eric looked at David and said, 'Are you in New York now?' It's the best definition of David Frost I've ever heard. We still joke that David has a convertible sports car and when it's raining he pushes a button on the dashboard and it stops.
3 Millicent Martin sang the now famous song to open the show and then left for Heathrow to catch a flight to Spain. We commented at the time that she'd probably land before the show had finished.

Partnerships

There are plenty of clever young writers. But there is too much genius, not enough talent.

J.B. PRIESTLEY[1]

'The Frost Report' used material from an eclectic bunch of writers, from Marty Feldman and Keith Waterhouse to Denis Norden and Bill Oddie. In those days, I always wrote in a partnership, and it was through Frost that I first met people like David Nobbs, Dick Vosburgh, Graham Chapman and Peter Vincent. I'm grateful, not only because I found my ideal working conditions but also because those people went on to become great friends as well. If there was any continuity in those partnerships, it was that I tended to work with people who were good at construction. I was good at punchlines, gags, stories, retorts, but not so good at what happens next. In terms of comedy writing, I became what the Americans describe as a 'lineman'. Often with my partners, we also fell into the roles of a walker, who paced up and down, and a sitter, who did the typing. For one thing, I remember the noise of the typewriter in those days was deafening. Today, when I write with Graeme Garden, I'm the one doing the pacing

---

1 He's ubiquitous.

and he's at his much quieter laptop, crafting ideas and dropping in his famously killer lines. I still prefer this dynamic. If you hit a blind spot on your own, you're stuck, but if someone else is there, something might happen. Ultimately, it's essential that you agree on what's funny. If you don't find someone else's material funny, you must say so. There's no point being polite. Another dynamic I've encountered, is that there is often a laid-back writer and a worrier. When I work with a musician called Ronnie Golden, he actually reckons that we're both laid back and worriers, all at the same time.

I think it's a truism of any kind of double act, whether they are writing or performing. Eric Morecambe and Ernie Wise were the classic example. Their image onstage was of the daft, carefree Eric and the serious, fretful Ernie. Behind the scenes, though, Eric was the worrier. He would fret as much about the annual Christmas show as he did about the weekly show on a Friday. Although he'd happily wiggle his glasses in his trademark style when approached by members of the public, Eric Morecambe was a shy man out of the limelight. He liked a good conversation but never felt the need to perform. He and Ernie came over to my house once for a party. Some stars are inclined to dominate proceedings at parties. Instead, it's rather telling that Eric spent the entire evening talking to a mate of ours. He was only interested in this man, who'd been left paraplegic by a rugby accident. Even so, he could have a slightly cruel streak when confronted with a member of the public (although nowhere near as prolonged as Tommy Cooper's legendary wind-ups); he was capable of devastating put-downs. I've told the following story many times before.[2]

Eric was once cornered by a man in a pub, who began pontificating on the subject of show business. Eric sucked intently on his pipe as the man wittered on, waiting for his moment. Eventually, it came.

'I always think,' said the man, 'that to be in show business you need three things . . .'

'If you've got three things,' interjected Eric, 'you should be in a circus.'

We invited Eric and Ernie back to the house a few years later, but Eric had been in hospital following a heart attack and couldn't make it. Ernie turned up, though, wearing a badge that said, 'He's very well, thank you.' That sort of sums up the partnership between Eric and Ernie. They cared very deeply for one another and although they were inextricably linked, they lived very different lives offstage. They needed the dynamic of a double act because neither wanted to be a soloist.

Eric was once talking to Billy Marsh, the agent who handled him, and he said, 'You know, Ernie and I always walk on together, every show. It gets monotonous. I've got an idea.'

Billy was intrigued. 'Go on,' he said.

'Well,' Eric said, 'it goes like this. Ernie and I come on separately and we never meet all the way through the show, except at the end.'

'That's very interesting,' said Billy, 'very interesting indeed. What a great idea.'

---

2 If this is your first time, you've got off lightly.

Eric paused. 'Actually,' he said, 'it's the worst idea I've ever had.'

Eric was relentless in his work rate. Maybe it was the fear of failure that drove him so hard. Rejection is a nasty fact of show business and no matter how many times it happens, you never quite get used to it. You still take it personally, even though you know that it's part of the game. I hew to Kingsley Amis's dictum to 'let it spoil your breakfast, but don't let it spoil your lunch'. You can always put the rejected script into a bottom drawer and use it for something else. Although you should always exercise this advice with caution, as the following story will illustrate.

Dick Emery once rang a writer and said, 'I've got a gap in the show, do you have any sketches I could have?' 'I'll see what I can do,' the writer replied, and as soon as he'd put down the phone he went to his desk and dug out a script he'd written for Tommy Cooper. As it had never been used, the writer knew that a few tweaks would make it ideal for Dick. So he dusted it off and passed it to a typist with the instruction that where it said 'Tommy' she should replace it with 'Dick'. The script was typed accordingly and then sent on to Dick, who immediately rang the writer.

'Very funny sketch,' he said, 'but I didn't really want your Tommy Cooper rejects.'

The writer blustered and attempted to protest, but Dick was having none of it.

'The giveaway is on the last page where it says, "Dick gives his characteristic laugh and his fez falls off."'

All that said, not all partnerships on 'The Frost Report' were fruitful ones. One afternoon, John Cleese and I sat down to write a sketch and it was a disaster. John and I were good friends but we were coming at the sketch from two different places. I wanted to write the whole thing in a kind of white heat and just finish the sketch. If it didn't work, I'd bin it and start again. John, on the other hand, wanted to analyse every single line of the first page before moving on. We laughed about it and went our separate ways. It was the same, later in my career, with Johnny Speight, the creator of Alf Garnett. We were once signed up to write an hour-long Frankie Howerd special together. We sat down to thrash out some ideas but it wasn't long before one of us[3] took off their glasses[4] to announce a surrender. Johnny was a lone wolf as a writer, a soloist, and we just couldn't make it work as a partnership. We agreed, instead, to write thirty minutes each and edit the halves together at a later date.

3 I won't say who.
4 Damn it.

Before Python

Those early Frost years saw the future Pythons cement the partnerships that would take them into the next decade. While we always felt something would happen to the group, it was hard to gauge exactly what that might be. Where John Cleese was immediately charismatic and possessed with star quality, the potential in Michael Palin wasn't so obvious at the time. Once again, my wife Terry showed her famous intuition with Palin: 'He can do anything,' she said, 'he's a straight man, a funny man – a real utility man.' Although I'm not sure that even she could have predicted that he'd become the next Alan Whicker. Terry Jones was the voluble and excitable Welshman, always having spats with John Cleese. However, you'd be surprised if disagreements within such a talented ensemble of people didn't happen. John used to say that it was because he was from Weston-super-Mare, and that West Country people didn't trust the Welsh. Luckily, there was a peacemaker and you won't be surprised to learn that this role was filled by Michael Palin. He hates the word 'nice', but he could walk into a room full of warring writers and performers and immediately calm everyone down. You can't do that if you're nasty. Eric was the lone wolf, who'd come out with these astonishing monologues full of verbal tics and tirades. It can't have been easy for him going up against two writing partnerships in John and Graham and

Terry and Michael, but his singular style got him through.

I subsequently worked with Eric on the Rutland Weekend Television spin off, 'All You Need Is Cash'. Eric used to joke that he filled the Rutland shows with 'Python rejects'. People sometimes ask me if I'd like to have written for, or even been in, Monty Python. I can honestly say that, although I was their warm-up man for a bit and played a couple of small parts in the TV series, the thought never occurred to me. I doubt the thought ever occurred to them either. In fact, the Python warm-up job is the only one I've ever sacked myself from.

'I'm not right for this because I'm a jolly joker and this show is a very different style. I'm wrong for it.'

John Cleese[1] looked rather surprised.

'Something we said, Barry?' he asked.

'Not at all,' I said. 'My style is grating on yours and I'm not right for the role. I'm not setting the right mood.'

They understood and, instead, I became a 'friend of the family'. I've never really hankered to be the kind of star that

---

1 One day in the mid 1970s I bumped into John Cleese in Soho. I asked him what he was up to and he told me that he was doing a sitcom. The sitcom format seemed far too straight for John, given everything he'd done in Monty Python, so I asked him what it was about. 'When we were filming in Devon with Python, we stayed at this hotel in Torquay. Well, the owner was quite an odd chap ...' I wished him luck with it, but I was unconvinced about the idea. And the rest is history. I should've known that if John was involved it would be something special. However, the critics were sceptical too and it took a while for them to love it. The same thing happened to Python. It was slotted in all over the schedule, at odd times of the night, and in some regions, it wasn't shown at all. No one could've predicted that there would be films and books and movie careers emanating from it. Well, I say no one. My agent Roger Hancock had some inkling that this new set-up might lead to something. John was with the Hancock agency in those days and Roger circulated a letter to all the other Python agents asking them to form a company to protect their clients' interests. For various reasons, the other agents weren't interested. So Roger formed Monty Python Productions by himself.

the Pythons became. I often wonder whether they did either. People know about me and I'm pleased about that, but that's as far up the ladder as I want to go.[2] I just feel lucky to have been around as long as I have. Although, you may like to know that my brief stint with Python didn't go completely unnoticed. I couldn't have been more pleased when Harry Shearer, star of 'Spinal Tap' and 'The Simpsons',[3] came up to me at the Edinburgh Festival[4] a few years ago and said 'Barry Cryer! Monty Python's warm-up man!' Apparently, Harry had been in England when those first shows were recorded and he'd seen me on the set. I guess you never know who's watching.

---

2 Ronnie Corbett once said to me, 'I don't know what rung of the ladder you're on, but stay there – no one's pointing at you.'

3 A man said to his doctor, 'I think I'm going deaf,' and the doctor said, 'What are the symptoms?' He said, 'They're that yellow family on television.'

4 Some years ago, Mel Smith was playing Winston Churchill in a play on the Edinburgh Fringe and the council said, 'You can't smoke that cigar onstage, otherwise we'll close the whole thing down.' Mel wanted to defy them but had to give in, playing with the cigar onstage but never smoking it. I was doing a show at the time in Edinburgh and I said, 'Portraying Winston Churchill not smoking a cigar is like portraying Bill Clinton with a sealed zip.'

Warm-Ups

I used to do quite a few warm-ups[1] in those days. I'd tell a few jokes, get the audience going, tell them what was happening and keep them entertained during breaks in filming. I once did a warm-up for the great humorist and musician Victor Borge. Although I'd seen him at the Palace Theatre, when I first came to London, and knew his material, I got in touch with the agent Tito Burns, to get Borge's CV. For the warm-up I went on and told the audience about his life story and career. I concluded with,

'The reason we're all here tonight is Victor Borge.'

The show began but the director called cut a few minutes in because a camera was down. Victor wasn't too pleased. He walked off and I was told to get on again. I told them that I was a bit uncomfortable telling jokes when people really wanted to see Victor. So I talked a bit more, trying to avoid telling jokes. Once the show was ready to start again, I repeated,

'The reason we're all here tonight is Victor Borge.'

He came back on and sat down at the piano. Then the

---

[1] A young comedian years ago at Granada TV was doing a warm-up and he got on to the subject of astrology. He said to the audience, 'Shout out your star sign and I'll tell you your main characteristics.' A man shouted, 'Aquarius.' The comedian quipped back, 'Big mouth, always wants to get in first.' Later on, the comedian was in the bar and the producer said, 'You're very good, I'd like to use you again. I loved that astrology joke you did.

'But how did you know somebody was going to shout Aquarius?'

camera problem happened again, and Borge's mood sank again. They wheeled me on and I was really stretching it this time. The problem was finally fixed and I said,

'For the third time, the reason we're all here . . . Mr Victor Borge.'

I backed off deferentially. Just before he made it to the spotlight he gripped my arm and said to the audience,

'Now you know why I'm here tonight. To fill in the gaps between Barry Cryer.'

The other great raconteur I did the warm-up for was Noël Coward, who was doing a face to face with David Frost at the Mayfair Hotel. I did my stuff to the audience, left the stage and then something similar to the Borge incident occurred and I was told to carry on. I walked back onstage, and noticed a bottle of champagne in a bucket of ice. I looked into the bucket and said,

'Monogrammed ice-cubes?'

It got me through an uncomfortable moment.

Graham Chapman

Of all the Pythons, I wrote most with Graham Chapman. He was wonderful with ideas and construction, whereas I was the lineman, able to get the characters to say something. At first it was Graham, Eric Idle and me, working together on sitcoms for Ronnie Corbett. Then Eric went off to work on programmes such as 'Do Not Adjust Your Set', and Graham and I carried on together, writing more than fifty TV shows. I loved working with him. He had a wonderfully sharp mind and could structure a gag brilliantly.

Unfortunately, later on, drinking started to hamper his work. He could still function but the time he spent working on new material became shorter and shorter. I would arrive at his house in Highgate at 10.30 a.m. and his hands would already be shaking as he poured the tonic. Around midday, he'd say rather offhandedly, 'Oh Ba, how about an early one?' We'd troop to the Angel Inn nearby and that would be it in terms of work. You can't function on an hour and a half's writing a day and while our friendship survived, the writing partnership dwindled. It saddened me a lot because I loved the man and I loved working with him.

One lunchtime, we went into the Angel with Keith Moon, the drummer of The Who and a notorious drinker and hellraiser. I thought we'd caught him on a day off, because I found him to be charming, friendly, quietly spoken and far from his 'Moon The Loon' image. Well, we were talking normally until Keith noticed that a few more people had entered the bar. 'Oh,' he said, with an air of resignation, 'I suppose they're going to want some Mooning.' And with that, he let out a terrible scream and threw his pint glass on to the floor. To my surprise, the management calmly ignored the incident. He sat down and we carried on talking as though nothing had happened. The people in the pub looked suitably impressed that they'd seen the legendary Keith Moon in action. Eventually we left, and just as we passed the bar Keith caught the barman's eye and said meekly, 'How much do I owe you for the glass?' Talk about breaking your image. Not long after Keith died, Graham and I went into the Angel at a time when he was on the wagon. I sat down and Graham went to the bar, returning with two pints. I was about to ask him why he'd bought himself a drink, when he threw his pint to the floor, glass flying everywhere. 'That was for Moony,' he said.

Frosty the Showman

In comparison to 'That Was The Week That Was', 'The Frost Report' was more thematic than satirical. We'd have a full writers' meeting at the start of the week, in a church hall in Crawford Street, Marylebone to discuss that week's topic. Anthony Jay would outline the thesis for the show and we would respond with what he called the 'Continuing Developing Monologue', or CDM,[1] which would knit that week's theme together. Then, after a game of football, we'd clear off to each other's houses to start work.

In 1967, the show won the prestigious Golden Rose award at the Montreux Festival and, to celebrate, we had a party at the Duke of Wellington pub over the road from the church hall. As the corks popped and the champagne flowed, Frosty noticed an older man who was sat, all alone on a barstool, watching the party in full swing. 'Mr Roy,' said Frosty, 'would you care to join us?' The old man's face lit up. He was brought over and introduced to us. His name was Harry Roy and he'd been a well-known big bandleader and clarinettist of the 1930s and 1940s. It was typical David: the memory for detail and the drawing in of people to make them feel special.

Frost also dealt very well with his critics, and was very

---

1 We would call it the 'Cadbury's Dairy Milk' and would try to ignore it as far as possible. We just wrote what we thought we could get away with.

skilled at steering them round to his way of thinking. We once came out of a studio at the same time that the audience was leaving. A man ducked under a rope barrier and marched up to David. 'Hello,' he said rather abruptly, 'I've never been to one of your recordings before. I always thought you were a charlatan and now I know you are!' David put his arm round the man and walked along with him. 'You won't believe what I'm going to say to you,' he said, 'but I'd like to thank you for your straightforward criticism. I'm surrounded by people telling me this show is wonderful and I hardly ever get the real view of the customers.' The man was now trying to speak but all that came out of his mouth were noises of apology. 'Don't mention it,' David interjected, 'I really mean it. Thanks very much, it's a tonic for me to hear it.' David lifted the rope and gently ushered the man under it. 'Thanks again,' he said, 'and goodnight.' Then David turned to me and mouthed a single word. A noun.

Frost didn't have it all his own way. There were still some people immune to his charms. Peter Cook told me that when he was the President of the Cambridge Footlights, David was the Secretary. Peter said that he only let Frosty run things because he was too 'bloody awful' to be in the sketches. However, Frost was tenacious. When the Footlights revue went on tour, Peter said that he pulled up to the theatre at Westcliff-on-Sea, to find that the poster read, 'David Frost presents ... The Cambridge Footlights'. Peter suspected David had been talking to the printer. Peter was once asked what his greatest regret in life was and, perhaps with this in mind, said 'saving David Frost from drowning'. This was a true story. In fact, at Peter's memorial, Alan Bennett got up and told the story of the rescue, ending with Peter's remark. David was in the second pew and he laughed his head off. It was a name check, after all, but you couldn't help thinking that the last laugh was Peter's.

Peter Cook

On a sunny Sunday morning a few months ago, I travelled to Greek Street in London's Soho to where the press had gathered outside a building. I hasten to add that they were not there for me, but for the unveiling of a memorial plaque to a revolutionary British comedy nightclub and its extra-ordinary founder. Quite an accolade when you consider that the club opened in 1961 and only ran for three years. The nightclub was the Establishment, the founder was Peter Cook and what a three years they turned out to be. Everything was changing at that time, the austere Fifties were giving way to the more carefree Sixties, and Peter and his club seemed to be right at the heart of it. If the Establishment was the club, *Beyond the Fringe* was the stage show, 'That Was The Week That Was' the TV show, and *Private Eye* the magazine. *Private Eye* was completely of the moment, despite being put together with Letraset in the bedroom of Willie Rushton's mother. There had been nothing like it before, and that goes for everything that was happening in and around Soho at that time.

Nevertheless, the 'old' Soho could occasionally manifest itself in the sizeable silhouettes of Maltese gangsters who ran practically everything. A couple of these characters visited Peter one afternoon, had a look round the Establishment and complimented him on the set-up. Peter was his usual charming and courteous self, buying the two men drinks and chatting to them happily. They left, and from that moment on, he didn't have any trouble from the Maltese mafia. No one knows exactly how Peter did it, but he was left alone to run his club. Perhaps the Maltese Godfather knew great talent when he saw it?

Peter was relentlessly funny. Those that knew him always said that he could walk into a room and if there was a cardboard box there, he'd be funny about the box. Comic ingenuity just poured out of him, even after the booze kicked in. Jonathan Miller said that he could stand about an hour with Peter before he had to leave. It's rather a distorted compliment, but he felt that he was just too funny. I was interested to read that in the 1970s, several police forces wanted to ban Pete and Dud's 'Derek and Clive' records. I think they show Peter at his best and his worst; pretty filthy but very funny. I think many of the problems between Pete and Dud were appearing at that time as some of the nastiness in those recordings feels very personal. It's safe to say that Peter was very jealous of Dudley's fame abroad. To him, he was just Dud from Dagenham and he couldn't work out why his old partner and friend was suddenly this major Hollywood film star. That level of fame never happened to Peter and it rankled. An American remake he did of 'Two's Company', the same show which starred Donald Sinden and Elaine Stritch over here, lasted only one series. I think he knew he wasn't an actor, but he was a fantastically funny man and one of the most amazing comics this country has ever produced.

Frankie Howerd

Although Dudley Moore was a regular at the Establishment, turning up to play modern jazz on the piano, Peter's booking policy at the club was eclectic. He would happily book the outrageous American comedian Lenny Bruce, and follow him with Frankie Howerd. Frankie's whole career was a rollercoaster, and the early 1960s saw it in something of a trough. The shows he did at the Establishment were a triumph,[1] real cult successes, and the first of a series of comebacks.

Frankie Howerd was an extraordinary character. I met him when I was a student in Leeds, and later on, I wrote for him several times. He had an agile mind that was able to turn in an instant from wit to cod-Latin and face pulling. Writers really enjoyed working for him because he always appreciated your efforts.[2] Even so, during a show, he liked to ad lib and would often point out what was his and what was the writer's. I think it was his way of having a measure of control over the material that was being written for him.

---

1 A live album was recorded and all you can hear during Frankie's spot is the cackling call of the Greater Spotted Kenneth Williams, disrupting proceedings as usual. At one point Frankie says, 'You're witnessing history, ladies and gentlemen – one comedian laughing at another.'

2 But mainly because you could include all the 'oohh', 'don'ts' and 'titter ye nots' on the page. If you were being paid by the page, a Frankie Howerd writing engagement could be a lucrative one.

Over time, he embraced every new generation of writers.[3] It was like a rite of passage, everyone wrote for him at some point. He enjoyed going to pubs and restaurants with us but, unlike his stage persona, he was rarely the life and soul of the party. Although he was very well read and interesting, we would often have the most marvellous conversation ruined by the introduction of depressingly serious subjects. Sometimes, after an evening with him, you felt like slashing your wrists. However, it's worth noting that he always generously paid the bill, something that wasn't always the case with other big names.[4]

After the Establishment club triumph, he was booked to do a short slot on 'That Was The Week That Was'. When he was still talking after fifteen minutes, Ned Sherrin, the producer, opted to let him carry on. Frankie's material was topical,[5] more topical than Eric and Ernie or Tommy Cooper would ever be, but he had this knack of reducing everything to a domestic level. Like Peter Cook, he'd often refer to Harold Macmillan, but he'd do it in such a way which made it seem like a gossip over a garden wall. Lady Dorothy Macmillan became Dot, and Frank would talk about Macmillan and then say, 'I blame Dot!' My mother was a fan. She used to say, 'He's like an old woman.' It was once pointed out that Frank didn't look like a comedian. He could wear the best suit and still looked like he'd slept in it. He could easily have passed for a member of the audience who'd

---

3 Sometimes literally.
4 Tommy Cooper was legendary for being close with a quid. We often joked that getting a picture of Tom getting in the drinks would be very valuable.
5 Frank once said to me, 'I've been doing the same act for forty years. I just change the names.'

managed to get onstage. The short-sleeve shirts and the crooked ties all pointed to a form of unthreatening eccentricity. This was reflected offstage too. Frank was very superstitious. One morning he went into the studio for a recording and the set was painted entirely green. He took one look at it and headed for the door, saying, 'I can't appear on it.' It had to be taken down and repainted in its entirety before he would agree to come back and record the show.

Frankie's bête noire was Larry Grayson. 'This man is doing my act,' Frank used to say. For example, Larry had a pianist that he patronised, as Frank did, but it was as much the differences as the similarities that infuriated him. One thing he didn't like was Larry's overtly sexual diversions about his friend 'Everard'. This was further than Frankie had ever gone in his act. The enmity was brought into focus when Bruce Forsyth left 'The Generation Game'. Frank was one of the first people on the phone telling Bill Cotton, the BBC's legendary head of light entertainment, that he would do anything to audition for the job. Now, Bill Cotton was a shrewd man who could see performers' limitations as well as their talents. He thought that while Frank was a great comic and a panellist, the job of host just wasn't right for him. To add insult to injury, it was Larry Grayson who got the job. Frank was somewhat displeased. Nevertheless, Bill was right. In the mid 1980s I was involved in a one-off version of 'The Gong Show', with Frankie at the helm and you could see that he just wasn't up to it. We did a couple of pilots that were shown late one Sunday night on Channel 4. It didn't discredit him, but he wasn't right for it. Frankie was the agitator, the abrasive element, not the avuncular host. He was too chaotic.

A very strange part of the Frankie Howerd story was Benny Hill's death. He and Frankie Howerd died the very same weekend in April 1992. Benny had been in hospital and was apparently back in his flat in Teddington when news broke that Frankie had died. The story goes that the press rang Benny's producer, Dennis Kirkland, to see if they could get quotes and Dennis decided not to bother Benny – because he'd been ill – and supplied some himself, which were printed as though from Benny.

Unbeknown to everyone, Benny was already dead. No one is quite sure when he died, but it's possible it was before Frank. He was discovered sitting in front of the TV, a curled-up sandwich and a stone-cold cup of tea by his side. The quotes that he'd 'given' on the death of his friend Frankie Howerd were posthumous.

Benny Hill had some of Kenneth Williams's reclusive qualities, but perhaps not quite as many of his hang-ups. Still, he lived an odd life for someone so revered as a comedian. He never owned a house and lived alone in a series of flats. He didn't drive and his agent, Richard Stone, would take him home after shows, but he'd never be invited in. I once bumped into Benny in Kensington High Street and you'd hardly have guessed he was a big star. He was wearing a cloth cap and a pair of nondescript glasses and was standing at a bus stop clutching a plastic shopping bag. Not a soul recognised him.

He was an enigma. He liked women, and would quite often invite one or two of his 'Hill's Angels', the famous troupe of attractive girls who starred on his show, round to dinner, but he was always the perfect gentleman and never made any attempt to chat them up. A taxi was called at the end of the evening and they went home, leaving him alone. A gourmet cook, he was known to rustle up a meal, concocted from damaged 'remaindered' cans from the supermarket. A celebrity chef, but one with an eye for a bargain.

I wrote the following poem for Frankie Howerd's memorial service, using many of his favourite catchphrases. I'm prone to writing poetry and I enjoy reading them out at various occasions, including memorial services.[6] Unfortunately, at my time of life, there seems to be rather a lot of them. Of which, more later.

Ode to Frank

Just make myself comfy ...
Once more unto the speech dear friends, once more
And sing in praise of Howerd, Francis
The tightrope walker who always took chances
Always wobbling, never falling
Captivating and enthralling
Confiding, chiding but never crawling
Fearful yet confident of his ability
Positively arrogant in his humility[7]
Making every line a sonnet
Please yourselves – don't take a vote on it
A true friend but not a sentimental man

6 After all, the show I do with Colin Sell, 'Clue's' resident pianist, is called 'Barry Cryer: Still Alive!'.
7 He was from Yorkshire, after all.

He was, to each lady and gentleman
Who enjoyed his friendship, which always lasted
Steadfast, never has my flabber been so gasted
I was amazed! When I realised how long it was in reality
He had beguiled us – such whimsicality
That face – someone called him King Leer and like
    Lear he depicted
To his audience of mad fools – a world where it was
    wicked to mock the afflicted
A world where pianists opined that it was chilly
With which he agreed, apparently willy-nilly
While confiding to us he was sweating like a pig
Frank was always in for a pound, infra dig
He could also inform us it was bitter out
Followed by a plea to get each titter out
That we could muster – oh folly, folly!
Such irrelevance – nolle prosequi? Not on your nolle!
That face – he defined as like a milkman's horse
To which my reaction was neigh, thrice neigh, of course
Crying: 'No don't laugh, it could be one of your own!'
This stand-up comedian stood alone
St Francis of Assisi – 'A Sissi? I heard that.' I can hear
    the retort
'How very dare you!' Never was haughty quite so haught
Such haughty culture – Bottom crossed with Puck
Yet ever reminding us 'Common as muck'
If that was common, may we all be so
He had common ground with us and we all know
With respect to E.M. Forster, there is no Howerd's End,
    that is not the case

At the risk of being naughty, shut your face
At this Eisteddfod, I shall go the whole hog
No epitaph, no epilogue. No. I joyfully conclude the
   prologue.

Kenneth Williams

It's amazing to think that before the Establishment club, Peter Cook wrote for a successful West End revue show called *One Over the Eight* while still at University. One of the stars of that revue was Kenneth Williams, the braying presence on that live Establishment recording of Frankie Howerd. People often expect comedians to be constantly turning cartwheels but more often than not they can be, at best, shy and, at worst, antisocial. Although the 'tears of a clown' syndrome can be a cliché, Kenny inhabited it better than most. Kenny was the definitive loner. His flat, if you were ever honoured enough to see it, was nothing short of frightening. He had no phone, no TV and there was nothing in the fridge. You weren't even allowed to use his loo. Instead, he would make you use the public toilet on the street outside the flat.

I knew Kenny from various panel shows, but I wouldn't say I ever really *knew* him. In company, he was an extrovert, telling all sorts of stories accompanied by that braying laugh. However, he harboured ambitions to be a serious actor and I believe that being typecast by the 'Carry On' series was the worst thing that happened to him. The persona he created for himself must have been a source of terrible frustration and anger. I remember meeting him occasionally at the Paris Theatre,[1] when we were waiting to take part in 'Just A

58

Minute'. I'd arrive and there would be Kenny, with his mum, Louie, waiting at the tea bar.

'Hello, mate,' he'd drawl, 'give us a fag.'

He never had any cigarettes on him, he always smoked OP's.[2] You'd pass him one and he'd say, 'And one for mum.' So there would be the three of us, puffing away and right on cue, Clement Freud would walk in, immediately grimace, and walk out again. Kenny knew that smoking wound him up. Clement would leave to the sound of Kenny's distinctive laugh.

Kenny was usually fuelled on rage during 'Just A Minute', which the audiences recognised and eagerly anticipated. Once, when I was a panellist, he suddenly took off on one of his flights of fancy and said, 'What was it 'amlet said, "oh that this too solid flesh would melt."' Immediately I buzzed and said, 'Lack of repetition. The line is, "Oh that this too, too solid flesh would melt."' Now, to a well-read man like Kenny this was a red rag to a bull and he was furious. 'Where do you find these buffoons?' he sneered, before tearing into me. On another occasion I started one of my minutes saying, 'One remembers ...' Kenny chipped in immediately, 'One remembers? One remembers? I don't remember.' 'Are you one, Kenny?' I replied, and for my efforts got the legendary 'death-ray' look. I don't think there was any malice in it, but as many of us were to discover when his diaries were

---

1 The Paris Theatre (also known as Paris Studios) was a former cinema located in Lower Regent Street, London, which was converted into a theatre by the BBC and used for those radio comedy broadcasts that required an audience. The BBC also used it to record live performances by artists such as The Beatles, Led Zeppelin and David Bowie. It closed in 1995, and was replaced by a purpose-built theatre in Broadcasting House.
2 Other People's.

published after his death, Kenny wasn't a man to cross. Ray Galton and Alan Simpson were astonished by what he'd written about his time working on 'Hancock's Half Hour'. They said he was terrific company at the recordings, a joy to be with, and always ready with a gag or a quip. Then he would go home and write about the terrible day he had, pouring bile on to Sid James and others.

His collected letters came out shortly after the diaries, and they were very different in tone and content. I reviewed the book for the *Mail on Sunday* and was amazed to see the diversity of people that he wrote to. He wrote one to the crew of a Royal Navy destroyer and it was full of camp and mock outrage. The letters were Kenny's public face. The diaries revealed the private side of a man who was full of bitterness, self-loathing, and disgust. He isolated himself with an obsessive sense of his own privacy. Being on show was addictive for him, and, if he knew he had an audience, he'd talk loudly and start acting up. He'd then get very acidic and you'd have to tell him that it was time to go home. The public face was of this wry little gnome with the great voices and anecdotes: the chat show host's dream. Unfortunately, that figure wasn't really there.

I remember the *Sunday Times* magazine once running a piece on the playwright Joe Orton and his boyfriend Kenneth Halliwell, who murdered him in 1967. It was a big, in-depth article illustrated by a huge photo of Orton and Halliwell on holiday in Morocco. In the middle, with his arms wrapped around the two of them, was Kenneth Williams. Kenny was horrified, and raged at how they dared to print such a private photograph.

My bridge partner

Tommy Cooper has left the building

Berkeley Square, 1853

Florence Nightingale

Woman with minivac

Two Ronnies writers' meeting

The windmill

The lovely Betty –
a stripper at the Windmill

My wedding
(day after)

BA Eng. Lit.
(failed)

Billy Connolly
(early years)

The baptism of
our eldest son

First luxury cruise

The great Snoop Dog

HIS MASTER'S VOICE.

Sell-out stadium tour
(day after)

Leaving the Priory

SDP conference 1984

Cabaret on the *Titanic* (went down well)

'As soon as you come out your front door you're in trouble,' he once said to me. 'We all have to go out,' I replied. 'No,' he said, 'not me. Trouble out there.'

Studio Days

Perhaps it would be better not to be a writer, but if you must,
then write.   J.B. PRIESTLEY

As I mentioned earlier,[1] once I'd become a Frost writer, a lot
of doors began opening for me and it wasn't long before I was
busily plying my trade for all manner of comedians. People
sometimes talk about the 1960s and 1970s as being a 'Golden
Age' of television. Firstly, I don't trust generalisations[2] and
I get frustrated with people of my generation who say that
we had the best of it, because that assumes that whatever is
on TV today doesn't bear comparison. There was a lot of
crap on TV back then,[3] and much of it has been forgotten
in favour of some great shows. Ultimately, I think it is an
arrogant point of view. I'd rather agree with Arthur Askey,[4]
who said that every generation is the same; there's a lot of
crap and a few brilliant people.

However, one reason I am pleased to have worked during
that period, is that we got to work for some great bosses. Bill
Cotton, Hugh Carlton Greene and Lew Grade, all let new
talent run. They not only let us get it wrong, but they
also let us live to write another day. There were many top-

---

1 p.32. You missed it? Stop flicking through this book and take it seriously. There'll
be questions later.
2 Especially generalisations about generalisations.
3 I should know, I contributed to some of it.

notch shows around then, and if anything has changed, I would say that it's a smaller pool now, despite the countless channels. There can't be another Eric and Ernie because the world has changed, having become less centralised. There is still a lot of comparable talent out there. It's just a case of finding it.

In recent years, I've spent a lot of time in studios and they've become very serious places indeed. Everyone knows their job and they're doing them with the highest degree of gravity. That's fine, and nothing beats getting on with the job with minimum fuss, but you'd be forgiven for thinking that they were making 'Newsnight', not a comedy programme.

Twenty or thirty years ago, studios in which comedy shows were being recorded were happy places, full of laughter and people enjoying themselves. We took the job seriously, because a show had to be made, but we never lost sight of the fact that it was entertainment. There are times now when I think people could afford to lighten up. However, I do remember that the two Ronnies were serious in rehearsal and would often learn the show off by heart. Technical runs were therefore solemn affairs, with the crew too busy con-

---

4 Arthur told a story about Coronation Day in London. Thousands of people were out, bands were playing, flags were flying, and there was a woman in the crowd who was triumphantly pregnant. A man said, 'Are you alright love? You look wonderful.' She said, 'Well they say it's twins.' To make conversation the man said, 'Oh I wish they could see all this.' And she said, 'Well I've taken my knickers off so they can hear the band.' Late on in his life, Arthur contracted gangrene and had to have his left leg amputated. I went to see him in St Thomas's Hospital in London and he was lying there laughing at a telegram sent by a friend. He showed it to me, and it said, 'I've booked a tour of Treasure Island with you as Long John Silver.' He loved that. When he lost his right leg as well, I went to see him again. This little man was lying there, the sheets flat out in front of him, and he's laughing again. He said, 'Do you remember that man who sent me the telegram? He's sent me another one – "Calm down, you've got the job."'

centrating on their cues to laugh, but none of this worried the Ronnies. When they got in front of an audience, there would be plenty of laughs and that's when it mattered.

Jack Benny

I was once working on a special with Des O'Connor and the legendary Jack Benny was appearing on it. Jack started his slot, but we ran out of recording time and Jack had to fly home the following day. Ever the professional, he changed the flight to the afternoon and came along, to a now deserted studio, the following morning. He did his bits to camera and left pauses in the middle of lines. Then he went into the sound box, where an engineer was adding the laughter. Most comedians would say, 'put the laugh where the punchline is' but not Jack. Instead, he asked that the laugh be placed just one beat ahead, because he knew that was when the audience would get the joke. When it was edited into the show, you couldn't tell the difference. A master class in comic timing from a master comic.

Peter Sellers

Peter Sellers had perfect timing, and to write lines for him was a pleasure. If he accepted them, that is. In the late 1960s, 'The David Frost Show' used to do two shows over a weekend, with the Sunday show being a bigger variety affair featuring top actors and singers. One week, word got round that we had Sellers booked for the Sunday show. We all started writing lines for him and he was presented with the material at rehearsal. He read brilliantly and it seemed all was well, but Peter was a mercurial figure. We completed what we thought was a perfect run-through, only to be told that he wasn't happy. Did we have anything else?

There was a certain amount of rushing around and digging into bottom drawers[5] before an alternative script was put together. He read it, and again he was brilliant. However, something still wasn't quite right, and he simply walked out of the building and went home. There was an uproar, because the show was that night, but no one was surprised. Peter had a quixotic reputation and he had driven many mad before us. To complicate matters he had an astrologer friend called Maurice Woodruff, and Peter found it very hard to make any decision about his life or career without resorting to Woodruff's advice. However, on this occasion, we were spared this kind of deliberation. Someone quickly got on the phone to him and asked him to come back. To his credit, he did just that. He came to the writers' room and asked for the stuff that we had done in morning. He read the first script and did it exactly as he'd done before. Having declared himself happy, the show went on. And yes, he was still brilliant.

---

5 Having heeded the 'Fez' warning on p.37.

Freddie Starr

Freddie Starr could be also mercurial, but his out-
rageousness quickly became part of his persona. As a result,
the writers and the crew treated him with a certain amount
of tolerance. He'd actually learned quite early on where
the line was, and as long as he didn't step too far over it
everything would be all right. In the early 1970s, I was
working with Dick Vosburgh[6] on an impressionist show
called 'Who Do You Do', which starred a host of great
impressionists including Freddie, Janet Brown, Peter Good-
wright and Paul Melba.[7] It was an edit show and there
were some recording nights when people wouldn't do as
much as others. The old pros accepted it as a restful night,
but Freddie, who was just starting to become really big,
didn't get it at all. One particular Friday night, Freddie
told one gag and suddenly walked past the cameras into
the audience, shouting, 'I'm the star of this fucking
show, but you wouldn't know it tonight, would you?' Jon
Scoffield, the producer, was blazing. 'Get him in here,' he
raged, and Freddie was ordered upstairs to the gallery. As
Freddie walked in, Jon grabbed him by the lapels and
shoved him up against the wall.

'Go home, little boy,' he said menacingly, 'you're finished

---

6 Of whom, much more later.
7 I was sitting in a restaurant one night when Freddie came in with Paul Melba.
They were standing at the bar, waiting for a table when Freddie shouted, 'You see
that fellow over there with grey hair and glasses, the one in the corner? It's Barry
Cryer. He has a lovely wife and he's a homosexual. She's got no idea and I think it's
very sad.' He was bellowing round the restaurant, so I went over and calmed him
down. Other people were alarmed by him but for some reason this was as far as his
practical joking with me ever got.

for tonight. Go home, come in tomorrow, and work!'

The following morning, Freddie was humble and contrite, shaking hands with everybody and apologising for his behaviour. Dick Vosburgh turned to me and said, 'I'm frightened, Barry. You knew where you were before. I think I preferred the old Freddie.'[8]

Oliver Reed

One of Freddie's mates at the time, Oliver Reed, had a similarly fearsome reputation on set. I met him backstage during the filming of a short-lived London Weekend Television show, hosted by Michael Parkinson, called 'All Star Secrets'. Having heard all the stories, I expected the worst, but that day Ollie appeared to be completely sober and we had a pleasant chat. Then he got the call that he was on next. With seconds to go, he pulled a grotesque face and staggered towards the studio. The other guests, including Henry Cooper and Wendy Richard, watched in horror as Ollie punched a hole in the set. Then he took a swing at Henry, and Wendy was so amazed that one of her false eyelashes fell off.[9] I couldn't believe what was happening. After the show, Henry came up to me and said, 'What was that all about?

8 There was another story about Freddie playing a club, which he turned up at with a heavily built minder. The club compere was on before Freddie and he was going down very well. Freddie thought, 'I have to follow this,' so he asked the man to come to the dressing room for a chat and he and the minder put the man in the shower and turned it on. The poor man had to get back on, drenched from head to foot, and introduce Freddie Starr.

9 I'm told that's a standard unit of surprise on chat shows. If Ollie had connected with Henry, perhaps both would've fallen off. We can but speculate.

The punch he threw at me was fake.– a perfect film punch.'
Henry then confided that if Ollie had actually punched him,
a certain amount of gentle upbraiding may have taken place.
Just how drunk was Ollie that night? I'll never know. It
certainly wasn't a great career move, because many film and
TV producers stopped booking him. A few years before the
Parky incident, Ollie was appearing on the Des O'Connor
show on Thames TV. It was produced by Philip Jones, who
was also head of light entertainment at Thames and our boss
on 'The Kenny Everett Video Show'. The chat show went
out live and because of Ollie's reputation, Philip went into
the gallery to keep a close eye on proceedings. He was greeted
by a close-up of Ollie, unzipping his flies and telling Des
that he wanted to show him his tattoo. 'All this, and Freddie
Starr to come,' groaned Philip. Funnily enough, Des's show
never went out live again.

Les Dawson

Before recordings of Les Dawson's show at the aforementioned Yorkshire Television studios in Leeds, David
Nobbs and I would invariably find him in the bar enter-
taining a group of people. It would take all our persuasiveness
to get Les back into the studio ready to film. Les was always
very giving of himself, and I now wonder whether this
selflessness may have had a detrimental effect on his health,
such was the untimely nature of his passing. My abiding
memory of him, though, was a man who loved words. Under-
neath the jolly exterior beat the heart of a writer.

'I was walking along the moors the other night, it must have been midnight. A man with a bale of cotton on his back approached me and said, "Is there an all-night mill in these parts?"'

Wonderful. Famously, Les used to play the piano deliberately out of tune, getting laughs when he hit a bum note and managed to keep a straight face. This led to speculation that Les was, in fact, a very good pianist. Les liked the idea that many people thought it took a special kind of talent to hit the wrong note at the right time. He liked people believing he could play brilliantly. Sorry Les, wherever you are, but that simply wasn't the case. I found this out when we decided to get Les and Humphrey Lyttelton together to do 'Bad Penny Blues', the jazz tune Humph wrote and made famous. They were both up for it as they had met recently and hit it off. Humph appeared in a couple of sketches, including one where he played Sherlock Holmes to Les's Dr Watson. Then we started to rehearse them for 'Bad Penny Blues'. We realised quickly that Les couldn't play the kind of boogie-woogie-style piano required for that song and he quickly became embarrassed. He wasn't a bad player, but I don't think he could play in the key that suited Humph's trumpet. We rewrote the whole thing so that Les talked to Humph and then slid off the piano stool to let musical director Laurie Holloway take over. We made a joke out of it but I think Les was a bit put out.

Tommy Cooper

Tommy was unique. I called him Mount Rushmore on legs.[10]
He had all the elements for a funny character, the fez, the
craggy face, the awful jokes and the botched magic, but he
also had that indefinable something that made him great.
What's not often mentioned is that Tommy would often
wind up members of the public who approached him. We
were once in a pub called the Britannia in Hammersmith
after rehearsals for a show. It was about 5.30 p.m. and all we
wanted was a quiet drink. A man came up to Tommy,
punched him on the arm.

'Tom! Can I tell you a joke?'

'Don't you know?' said Tom.

The man, somewhat hesitantly, started.

'These two men go into a pub . . .'

'S'cuse me a minute,' said Tom.

He leaned over the bar.

'Do you have a piece of paper?' he asked.

'Yes, Tom,' said the barman.

'Sorry,' said Tom to the man. 'Do go on.'

'Right. There were these two men in a pub . . .'

'S'cuse me, have you got a pen?' This, again, to the
barman.

'These two men go into a pub.'

'Sorry,' said Tommy, 'is the name of the pub important?'

'No,' said the man, bemused. 'It's just any old pub.'

Laboriously, Tommy wrote down 'any old pub' on the

---

10 Not to his face, obviously.

paper. A knot of people had now gathered to see what he was up to.

'So,' he said, 'these two men in a pub – what do they do? Are their jobs important?'

'No,' the man replied.

Tom wrote 'jobs not important' on the paper. He let the man run for a little longer, interrupting him another couple of times. Just as the punchline was approaching, Tom spotted a cameraman he knew walking through the pub door.

'Harry,' he said. 'Come here. You've got to hear this.'

Tom turned to the man.

'Sorry, do you mind starting again?'

As the man cleared his throat to start again, Tommy walked out of the pub. Unfortunately, this wasn't the first time that I witnessed this sadistic streak. Ultimately, Tommy sulked if he couldn't be the centre of attention. I hear of another evening where Tommy was in a pub that divided into two rooms. A man shouted out a greeting to Tommy from one room and began telling him a joke. Tommy pretended to listen intently, whilst undoing his belt. Half the pub is in hysterics because they can see Tommy Cooper dropping his trousers and the other half is in hysterics because they can see Tommy Cooper being laughed at. Meanwhile, this poor man is in the middle, thinking the joke is going enormously well.

Mike Yarwood told me that he and Tommy Cooper were once in separate Blackpool shows and often used to dine together afterwards. One night, a man joined them, uninvited. The man ordered steak and mashed potatoes. When all the meals arrived, the man noticed the waiter had brought chips instead of mash. The waiter left and the man declined to make a fuss but Tommy insisted that he get what he ordered. Tommy beckoned the waiter over and told the man to say something.

'Erm, I didn't order chips with this,' the man said sheepishly. 'It was actually mash that I wanted.'

'Stop making a fuss,' Tommy butted in, 'you're embarrassing everybody. Eat your chips!'[11]

Tommy didn't just reserve this behaviour for members of the public. Freddie Starr told me about a charity show he did with Tommy in Liverpool. Freddie was in awe of Tommy, and thrilled just to be on the same bill. He was even more pleased when Tommy asked him to join him and his wife, Gwen, for tea that afternoon in the lounge of the hotel they were all staying in. Now, as we know, Freddie could be outrageous and Tommy was aware of this. He warned Freddie that he would stand for no swearing, especially in front of Gwen. Suitably chastised, Freddie arrived at the hotel, all scrubbed up and as polite as a public schoolboy.[12] Freddie stretched out a hand.

'Hello, Tom. Hello, Mrs Cooper.'

---

11 You'll be pleased to know that the public can occasionally get their own back when confronted by well-known entertainers and their egos. There used to be an informal club of actors who took the famous Brighton Belle train up to London Victoria and would return the same evening. Donald Sinden tells the story of a group of actors on this very train one morning, laughing, swapping stories and trading gossip as they headed to London. A man approached their table, uninvited, and asked if he might join them. The actors budged up for him and he told them that he 'was in pressed steel'. For a whole five minutes the man talked about his business and bored them rigid with news of all the latest innovations in the industry. The actors sat open-mouthed. He stopped, and stood up. 'Wasn't that interesting?' he said, 'about as interesting as listening to you lot laughing and shouting.' 'That man had style,' said Donald, 'so much so that I wanted to clap!'

12 Whether this was before or after his encounter with Jon Scoffield, I can't say.

'Fuck off,' said Tom.

Bizarrely, Tommy would rarely talk about the real world and he certainly never made small talk. If the conversation did turn serious, the cards would come out and he'd do close-up magic and tell jokes. He once said to me, 'There are a hundred good magicians in the country, and I'm the idiot.' He was good, and he knew it, but this meant that he wasn't easy to write for. He was hopeless in sketches because he never remembered cue lines as he would take a basic script and just run with it. The ideal sketch for Tommy Cooper would go something like this: Tommy enters tailor's shop, does trousers jokes and exits. He could create brilliance out of something simple.[13]

---

13 When Jerome Flynn played Tommy, in the stage show *Jus' Like That*, he resisted doing an imitation of Tommy. I knew Tommy very well and I thought Jerome's take on him was brilliant. He came the closest to capturing this essence of brilliance. In my opinion, that show should've run for far longer than it did. We can all do a Tommy Cooper to some degree, but Jerome really seemed to have stepped inside him and it was quite weird watching it happen. When it started, I thought he didn't really look much like Tom (although he had the chin) but within minutes I was in, and transfixed by his performance. As I told him afterwards 'You didn't become Tommy Cooper; Tommy Cooper became you.' Perhaps a little trite, but I meant it.

Dick Vosburgh

> If you are a genius, you'll make your own rules, but if not –
> and the odds are against it – go to your desk no matter what
> your mood, face the icy challenge of the paper – write.
>
> J.B. PRIESTLEY

In the business I'm in, it's very easy to become pedantic about words. It's not just how some words are abused that bothers me, but also how often these words are abused in the wrong context, so as to dilute their original meaning. One such word is 'genius'. I've heard it said about so many people in so many different situations, I now switch off when the term is applied. It's become such a devalued word and yet, just very occasionally, I've encountered people who come pretty damn close to matching its description. Unequivocally, this applies to Dick Vosburgh, and I'll introduce him by way of a poem I wrote about him:

A Man for All Reasons

Greetings.[1]
It's impossible, not just hard,
To emulate the bearded bard

---

[1] For those that didn't know him, this was Dick's customary salutation, delivered in his unmistakeably honeyed, RADA tuned, New Jersey tones.

There is no secret – there is no trick
There was only ever one Dick
How to start my panegyric
About a man with soul satiric
The maestro of the flawless lyric
Dear Dick's voice now clearly chimes
In – enough already with the triple rhymes
So I desist – he was the one
Over forty years of fun
Always major, never minor
Every breath a great one-liner
It's quite difficult, I swear it's true
To have an old friend who's an idol too
Enough already! It's time to leave it
Dick's not gone, I don't have to believe it
Alright alright, that voice so mellow
I think that's quite enough my fine fellow
So let's make this the happiest of meetings
End as I began to you all and Dick – greetings.

Dick Vosburgh was probably not only the funniest person I've ever known, and I've known a few, but he was also one of the most underrated. He could sing, act and write anything from one-liners to music, lyrics, sketches, musicals, plays and even obituaries. He was an extraordinary character.[2] I knew him for more than forty years and every minute spent in his company was a pleasure.

---

2 Once described as 'Dorothy Parker with a beard'.

Dick was an American, born in New Jersey, and while he never lost a trace of his accent or his distinctively American way of looking at life, he was also an Anglophile. He came to Britain to study at RADA and it was there that he met Beryl, who would later become his wife. He had ambitions to become an actor but although he was in a few stage plays, the break never came. Luckily, especially for those of us who worked with him, Dick made the move into writing. It was something he'd always talked about doing, but never addressed until his acting ambitions sputtered out.

For all those people who believe the old saying that the pram in the hall is the death of art, let me tell you that Dick had no less than six children, all crammed into a tiny place off Sloane Square that was filled with piles of books and papers, and he still managed to write the most wonderful material. If the domestic set-up ever got too much, Dick would simply wander down to the nearest Tube station and, possibly accompanied by one or more of his children, get on the Circle Line. There he would sit all day, writing, while the train looped endlessly round. Even when they moved to Islington, the Vosburgh world seemed to be one of organised chaos. I remember once going round for a meal and, as usual, Dick was eloquently enthusing about something. He casually put his plate of food to one side and I watched, half-fascinated and half-horrified, as the family cat wandered over, had a good chew, and cleared off. I pointed this out, but as Dick was busy expounding, he hadn't noticed a thing. Beryl said that he wouldn't notice if a riot was going on around him. He often spent a lot of time at the British Film Institute library and was always carting an armful of books around.

Beryl and I once imagined him wandering up Tottenham Court Road during the Poll Tax riots of 1990, with broken glass everywhere and police sirens at full blast. Beryl might say, 'Did you get caught up in the riot?', to which Dick would growl 'What riot?' in that lovely bass baritone.

I met him in the early 1960s. I'd heard about him, and I was pleased when I found out I would be working with him on a TV show called 'Stars and Garters', which was a variety show set in a pub. Dick and I hit it off straight away. The chemistry was there from the start and we went on to write scores of shows together. Although unusually for one of my partnerships, Dick wasn't that good at construction, so I had to learn quickly. Dick's lines were just so lovely and they poured out of him, so much so that I could hardly keep up with him. I wrote them down as best I could and tried to get them into some sort of order.

He loved one-liners but above everything else, Dick was a lyrics man. He relished great lyricism and adored Cole Porter, Irving Berlin and Rodgers and Hammerstein. Dick was once working with Ronnie Corbett where Ron had to rehearse an old Cole Porter number. Ron said to Dick, 'What a shame there are only three verses. I'd love to do a fourth.' So Dick went away and came back with the fourth verse. Ron said you couldn't tell the difference.

Perhaps he was so underrated because everything he wrote had an American slant. I always thought that he'd have been more successful if he'd stayed in the United States. I could imagine him working on something like 'The Sid Caesar Show', where he could come up with the endless zingers typical of those big shows. However, he loved Britain tremendously and, once he had a wife and family, it was difficult to return.

Towards the end of Dick's life, I received a call from my agent telling me that Jackie Mason, the great American stand-up comedian, wanted to revive *Hellzapoppin.* I'd met Jackie Mason and I thought it would be a lot of fun to work with him. This old 1930s revue show had not only been a huge hit on Broadway, but it was also later turned into a film. I thought it had Dick Vosburgh written all over it. I mentioned it to him and he was immediately interested. Sadly, for various reasons the deal was never signed. The contract came through but money issues were involved and it just wasn't going to happen. It was a real pity because I was very much looking forward to it, even though I knew I'd be a passenger once Dick came on board and did his wonderful thing. If he was disappointed, which I'm sure he was, he never showed it. We were very much of the same mind – if it isn't happening, move on to something else.

Dick was so naturally witty that he often had the right words in the oddest of locations. We were once in the gents' toilet at Thames Television and Dick was sounding off about the producer of a show we were currently working on. I looked round and noticed there was an 'engaged' sign on one of the cubicles. I nodded to Dick to indicate that he was being heard and, without missing a beat, said, ' …and those are my sentiments, as sure as my name is Barry Cryer.' Another time, a woman came up to us in the bar at London Weekend Television and obviously recognised Dick. 'Oh Mr Vosburgh,' she gushed, 'you're so wonderful! How do you do it?' He smiled, replying, 'I hold, as t'were, a mirror up to nature.'

Dick was a great bear of a man and sported a large beard, which was black in its heyday. He once took part in a long-forgotten game show called 'Whose Baby?' in which the children of famous people came on and you had to guess who the parent was. The host said to one of Dick's daughters, 'Who looks most like your father?' 'Rasputin,' replied the little girl. Dick was so proud of her.

I appeared in *A Saint She Ain't*, which was Dick and Dennis King's homage to the great Hollywood movies of the 1930s and 1940s. In true Vosburgh tradition, it liberally parodied stars from the time, and I was asked to play a W.C. Fields-style character. One of my recurring nightmares is that I will forget my lines. I'm no stage actor, and I have tremendous admiration for those people who can go on and stand in the same place and recite the same lines, night after night, month after month. I watched them every night during *A Saint She Ain't* and I was in awe. In the cast was Michael Roberts, who played a character based on Lou Costello, and he and I would sometimes have a little fun with the script. There was one particular line that he would change each night, and I'd reply to it with something of my own. We actually got told off for doing this, and quite rightly too, because there were actors waiting for their cues. In fact, Vincent Marcello, who was playing a character styled on Bud Abbott, grabbed my arm one night and I could see the panic in his eyes. He had no idea what we were going to do next. Luckily, the moment passed and the show carried on, but Michael and I agreed to tone it down after that. Most of my scenes were with the wonderful Wirral comedienne Pauline Daniels, who played a Mae West-type role. When the musical transferred to the Apollo on Shaftesbury Avenue, they suggested that only my name should be put up in lights outside the theatre. However, Pauline was playing the main role, and it wouldn't have felt right if I was up there in lights on my own. I'm pleased to say that she got the recognition she deserved, because she was fantastic. In fact, the reviews for the show were very good and I was tremendously pleased for Dick.

Dick was also an expert on the McCarthy era of American history, when that dreadful government committee, simply because of political leanings, ruined the lives of many good people. Dick's show, *The Un-American Songbook*, again written with Dennis King, was a mixture of old standards and new songs written with wonderfully ironic lyrics. It was written for a cast of four and it was a brilliant show. One of the cast members was an American character actor called Johnny Meyers, who stepped out of character at one point in the show to talk about his father, a schoolteacher who fell foul of the McCarthy committee. It was very moving to hear how the family had to keep moving to escape persecution, and it showed up just what a horrible era it was for many people.

That show was the last thing Dick did. He looked very gaunt at the final performances but he was still Dick – funny, witty and indomitable. Even in hospital, where he was being treated for cancer, he could crack jokes. One night, they had to anaesthetise him for a routine check and, when he came out of it, he saw a nurse looking at him with concern.

'Are you all right, Mr Vosburgh?' she asked.

'Is it a boy?' he replied.

Genius is a word that is often applied without merit, but not when it comes to Dick. He could make the kind of leap of imagination that takes a person from the ordinary to the brilliant. He was a master of all that he did, and I'm very proud to have known such an amazing person. I miss him tremendously.

Ray Cameron & Kenny Everett

Ray

I met Ray Cameron when I hosted a show for Yorkshire Television that Ray and Mike King devised called 'Jokers Wild', which ran from 1969 to 1973. It was freely based on an American radio show called 'Can You Top This?'. Ray and Mike tweaked the format from three to six comedians and added a host. I had this little machine that showed a subject category every time I pressed a button, and whoever's turn it was would tell a joke. The point of the game was that the other panellists could interrupt with a joke on the same subject. It didn't always work that way, and there was a lot of fun based around completely irrelevant interruptions. As a format for a game show, it worked a treat and we used a good mixture of the old heavyweights, including Ted Ray, Les Dawson and Arthur Askey, and younger comedians.

Some time after 'Jokers Wild' had finished, Angela Bond, the veteran radio producer, invited me to lunch with Kenny Everett to talk about doing a radio series together. We hit it off immediately and although that show never happened, it was obvious that Kenny had the potential to be a big star. Kenny was already a hit on radio and I thought his uniquely talented personality would transfer well to TV. However, it took the advice of the eighteen-year-old son of the head of light entertainment at Thames Television, Philip Jones, for Kenny to get his break. When that happened, I was called in as a scriptwriter, and there was a meeting with David Mallet, the producer and director of 'Jokers Wild'.[1] David and I would be working on a segment of Kenny's new show, which was a scaled-down game show. Immediately, we thought that Ray Cameron would be perfect for the show and it wasn't long before he was brought on board. He and I went on to write all the Everett shows for Thames and later the BBC.

Ray was highly creative and innovative. He'd watched a lot of US TV whilst growing up in Canada and he'd gone on to become a stand-up.[2] The original premise of the show was essentially an extension of Kenny's radio show. Kenny, as a kind of proto DJ, would introduce bands and singers and comment on them. Ray knew how comedy and music might cross over and he introduced a wealth of verbal and visual ideas that suited Kenny's style. The bits that Kenny did between the music became longer and longer, and almost without realising it, we'd created a comedy show with musical guests instead. Cliff Richard, Rod Stewart, Bryan Ferry, David Bowie and Freddie Mercury, among many others, queued up to be humiliated and cheerfully insulted. They knew the score and they all really went for it.

In the mid 1980s, Ray and I worked on a show called 'Assaulted Nuts' for HBO in America and Channel 4 here. It was a sketch show that mixed American and British performers. Among them was an up-and-coming comedy actress called Emma Thompson. Unfortunately, when the second

---

1 He also directed Peter Kay's memorable 'Amarillo' video for Comic Relief.
2 In fact, he once opened for the Rolling Stones.

series came round, Emma couldn't do it, so we got the obvious replacement, Tim Brooke-Taylor. Among the Americans was Bill Sadler, who subsequently appeared in *Bill and Ted's Bogus Journey* and *The Shawshank Redemption*, and Wayne Knight, who later popped up in *Basic Instinct*, *Jurassic Park* and was Newman in *Seinfeld*. It was a very happy time, because I was working with an expert like Ray and indulging my own passion for American humour.

Ray was a man of big ideas and bigger plans and he eventually finished up in Washington State having married an American. We had a theory that he was slowly making his way back to Canada. Our parting as a writing team was amicable and I wished him all the best of luck with his new life abroad. I was hugely fond of Ray and I miss him very much. I could hardly keep up with his ideas, which is such a huge asset working in television. Quite recently, I had a call from Ray's son, Michael McIntyre, the stand-up comedian. To me, he had always been 'little Michael', who used to visit the studio as a five-year-old and share jokes with Kenny. Mike came over to my house and we talked for five hours non-stop. I think his dad would have been hugely proud of Michael's success.

Ev

God only knows what commissioning editors of today would make of someone like Kenny Everett. First of all, Kenny was not a comedian in the conventional sense. He had no preconceived ideas of what he 'ought' to be doing. I think this is what helped us break so much new ground with him. He was just Kenny – daft, funny, brilliant, witty and always open to ideas. Amazingly, he also just happened to be making a high-profile show for a mainstream TV channel that attracted millions of viewers.

Kenny[3] was marvellous at taking characters that Ray and I created for him and bringing something completely unexpected to them. For example, when we were doing Kenny's show for Thames, we had a character called Brother Lee Love, a black-hatted American preacher with huge polystyrene hands, who used to come on to the backing of a gospel choir. One day, completely unscripted, Kenny threw off the fake hands, grabbed the autocue camera and spun it round to face the rest of the studio. All the usual detritus of a working studio was revealed; the dirty walls, the cups of coffee and the crew scurrying about with clipboards. To the amusement of everyone, Kenny looked down the barrel of the lens and said, 'Oh, the glamour of it all!' For a moment he'd stepped out of character and given the viewers a brief insight into what making TV was really all about. It was a pure Spike Milligan moment. We left it in the show and when it was broadcast, it drew a lot of attention.

In 1981, Kenny left Thames and signed a new deal with the BBC. Everyone was very excited by the move, but Ray and I quickly became suspicious that the BBC was trying to turn Kenny into a 'BBC' comedian. We were doing a pre-record one afternoon and I said to Kenny, 'Do the camera

---

3 Kenny Everett used to have a very interesting take on various aspects of modern life. He once said of the video recorder: 'Oooh, the end of now as we know it.' He said it was a status symbol, and that if you asked a person with one if they'd seen a particular programme the night before they'd say, 'Not yet.'

gag again.' So he did exactly the same thing, pulling the camera around to reveal the distinctly unglamorous studio, and repeated the line he'd previously used. Bill Wilson, the producer, came down from the gallery.

'Very funny,' he said. 'But could we do it again? There was a shadow on Kenny's face.'

'We do tacky, Bill,' I said, 'let's leave it as it is.'

The BBC soon wanted the script in advance and any hint of roughness, which we thought was an integral part of Kenny's show for Thames, was quickly excised.

Kenny's was the only show I worked on where no one said 'quiet' before the cameras started to roll. All the laughter you could hear was from the crew and was totally genuine. We invented a character called Sid Snott, who was an ageing rocker dressed in black leather. Kenny used to flick fags towards his mouth as he was speaking, never quite managing to catch them. One day, he caught one, and he was so surprised that he almost started laughing. He just about managed to contain himself and instead he ate the fag before walking off. The laughter that accompanies this particular piece of unscripted Kenny is wonderful to hear.[4]

As I write, I'm in discussions to be involved in a new stage show about Kenny's life. As a result, I've been having a look at some of the old clips from the show. I'm delighted to say that everything still feels fresh, very funny and only the bands

---

4 Although we'd almost invariably have a live audience in those days, I admire comedy which doesn't depend on an audience providing a laughter track, 'The Royle Family' being a perfect example.

date it. One clip I watched features Cliff Richard,[5] in what looks like an old piece of black and white footage. He's singing away until Kenny strolls into the frame wearing a bright red shirt and blue jeans. 'Get out of my old clip!' says Cliff. With careful wardrobe and make-up, we'd got Cliff to look pretty much as he did in the late 1950s. I was very proud of that sketch.

Off-screen, Kenny was usually quite shy but once he warmed to a theme, he'd become more playful. We used to go to a Chinese restaurant on the Goldhawk Road to wind down after the show, and Ev became fascinated by a plaque on the door of the gents, which featured a figure of a dancing man, complete with top hat and cane. One night, we sat down to order our food and Kenny announced that he needed to visit the loo. He pulled out a top hat and cane and danced down the restaurant.

In the mid Sixties, Kenny married Lee Middleton, but they eventually separated and Kenny came out as gay. When Lee remarried, Ev was invited to be the best man. At the reception he got up to speak, looked at the groom and said, 'For God's sake don't tell her about us!' He loved women, and was very close to Cleo Rocos, the improbably curvy Brazilian model who used to guest on the show.[6] The crew particularly looked forward to the filming days that involved

---

5 He was a regular guest. Kenny could pull in some very big names. Freddie Mercury took time out from a world tour just to be on the show. Kate Bush did a 'Mastermind' spoof, where she answered all the questions out of sequence (with thanks and apologies to David Renwick, who perfected the art on 'The Two Ronnies'). In an interview sketch, I got Bryan Ferry to answer all of Kenny's questions as languidly as he could. These were big stars, but they all wanted to be on 'The Kenny Everett Show'.

6 Usually in her underwear.

her,[7] and she was treated like one of the team.[8] One day, Kenny told me that he and Cleo had got engaged. I could barely believe it, as we all went out to a restaurant that evening to celebrate. However, Kenny didn't mention the engagement with any seriousness, instead treating it like some kind of joke. I think Cleo was upset, because she loved Kenny very much.

Kenny had an amazing gift for learning lines after only a couple of run-throughs of a sketch. It used to unnerve some of the actors we'd hire, that Kenny didn't know the script when they arrived. I remember the great Geoffrey Palmer once turned up to do something on the show and, like the professional he is, he'd learned all his lines. Geoffrey was slightly worried to see that Kenny had an autocue as he thought it would look like he was reading. However, after rehearsals, Geoffrey was amazed at the speed with which he could pick it up. Not so Spike Milligan, who arrived one afternoon to be greeted by the same set-up. 'I've been up all fucking night learning my lines,' he complained. Everett then arrived in the studio and greeted one of his idols. 'Everett,' muttered Spike, 'remind me to send you an assassin for Christmas.'

---

7 Because she was usually in her underwear.
8 One of the team that was usually in her underwear.

Pubs

A doctor was in a pub relaxing when a man came up and said, 'I know you're off-duty, I must apologise for bothering you, but I'm getting this frightening migraine right across my forehead and my GP hasn't managed to do anything about it. Have you any suggestions?' And the doctor said, 'I had that, and the aspirins and pills didn't seem to do anything. One night I was in bed with my wife and I put my head between her breasts and the headache disappeared and has never happened again. Give it a go.' Three weeks later they met again in the pub, as people do in jokes, and the doctor remembered the man and said, 'How's your headache? Did you do what I suggested?' 'I did,' replied the man, 'and haven't you got a lovely home?'

My time working for David Frost marked the transition in my life from performer to writer. I didn't really think too much about it at the time as it was so seamless. The great thing about writing, of course, is that you can do it anywhere. These days, I always work in the kitchen at home despite the fact that I have a study upstairs. I like the distraction; the radio on, the children (now the grandchildren) running about and my wife Terry busily going about her day. I don't need solitude. I'm a terminally gregarious peopleaholic.[1]

---

[1] And if you can find that sentence anywhere else in world literature, I'll give you a fiver.

I also have an office in central London. If I'm working on a script I prefer to be at home, but sometimes I need to hold meetings in central London. However, I'm not a huge fan of eating curled-up sandwiches in sterile, soulless offices and PowerPoint presentations are not really my thing. Instead, my office is very convivial and extremely well placed in Langham Street. It's also very convenient if you happen to be at BBC Broadcasting House. It's a pub called the Yorkshire Grey[2] and I like to tell people that it's named after me. I enjoy meeting old friends and colleagues there.[3] Normally, the traditional BBC pub of choice for after-show gatherings or informal meetings is the George in Mortimer Street but I discovered this alternative a few years back.[4]

Meetings and social gatherings in pubs are one thing, but

---

2 When Dylan Thomas was doing a lot of writing for BBC radio, he was frequently in the George. One afternoon, as he was drinking with a gang of BBC people, a regular burst through the door. He told the group that a man whose wife Thomas had been 'escorting' behind his back, was approaching the pub. 'He's coming to get you,' panted the informant. With that, Dylan lifted the hatch and scuttled under the bar as the cuckold roared into the pub. 'Where's that bastard Thomas?!' roared the cuckold as Dylan cowered beneath the pumps. The Grey regulars began clucking around the distraught man, offering sympathy and alcohol as he poured out his heart about his wife's affair with the legendary poet. Eventually he calmed down and got on to another subject. As he did so, an arm emerged from under the bar, found the pint that it was clutching only minutes previously, and carefully took it back down. And if it isn't a true story, then it should be.
3 Including Russell Davies, the broadcaster, musician and general encyclopaedia of jazz. He's very quick, as I found out one afternoon when I made a joke about 'Placebo' Domingo – 'who does nothing for me'. Like lightning, Russell retorted, 'and of course "Flaccido" Domingo, who does nothing for anyone.'
4 It even has its own special code. When someone inside Broadcasting House asks, 'Where are they?' the reply comes back 'in Studio YG1'. The same trick was used at the Old Coffee House pub in Beak Street, Soho, where any performer who had just popped out for refreshment could be innocently described as having 'nipped to the coffee house'. Lower case, of course.

working in them is quite another. It's worth mentioning at this point, that in the early part of my career, pubs played a greater part in a writer's working life than they probably do now. I wouldn't want to give you the impression that I visited pubs for any other reason than they were just part of our professional fabric.[5] Besides, pubs are great places for people-watching and anyone looking for writing inspiration could do worse than sit in one for a couple of hours. David Nobbs and I went into a pub in the Goldhawk Road, Shepherd's Bush, after rehearsals for a show we were working on. David sat down and I went to the bar. The barman said he had to get something from the cellar and he disappeared. There was a couple behind me, talking very seriously, and I couldn't help listening in to the conversation. Bearing in mind that this was when a 'trannie' meant a radio, the conversation went something like this:

Woman: I'm sick of you wanting to get a trannie. Sid's got some at trade price.

(Pause)

Woman: So I'll get one from Sid and you can pay him when you see him.

(Pinteresque pause)

Man: I'm still annoyed about leaving my hat in the office.

The feeling that went into that long pause, and the non sequitur that followed it was wonderful. I love random snatches of conversation like this. The kind you hear in

---

5 Oh, go on then. Just the one.

public places, like on buses or in the street, are priceless. They are little fleeting moments that can often say so much. A while back, the *Guardian* newspaper sent five people to hang about in public places, listen to people talking and bring back the results. My favourite was from a garden centre, where a man was overheard saying that the sundial he bought last year had 'paid for itself already'. I immediately rang Alan Bennett,[6] because we have a shared love of these sorts of snippets. When Alan finds something very funny, he doesn't laugh. Instead, he produces a sort of groaning sound and if you're with him, he takes off his glasses and wipes his eyes. Needless to say, when I read this out to him over the phone, he groaned heartily.

It becomes a little trickier in pubs if you yourself become the subject of attention. Years ago, my writing partner John Junkin and I went to a pub in Hatch End, where I live, called the Railway. We were planning to do some work and so we bagged a table right at the back, and got down to writing. Almost on cue, a man came over and began asking us what we were doing. Now, you don't mind the odd polite inter-ruption but this man had barged in and was making a nuisance of himself. Junkin and I were silently trying to work out a way to get rid of him, when across the floor came Brian Whitehouse, a BBC producer and a Railway regular. 'Do

---

6 In America they changed the title of Alan Bennett's *The Madness of George the Third* to *The Madness of King George* because they thought that the audience would assume it was a sequel. When it was a play at the National, I told Alan that I'd been at a dinner party and somebody was talking about a play they'd seen. 'What did you see?' I was asked. '*The Madness of George the Third*,' came the reply. Suddenly, from the other end of the table, a woman piped up, 'What was that about Thora Hird?' I got a handwritten card from Alan which said, 'Rehearsals have just commenced for the Madness of Thora Hird. The curtain rises to the clash of zimmer frames.'

you mind?' he said, 'these people are working.' Brian then simply took the man by the elbow and steered him to the front door. Although pubs are public places, Brian obviously thought the man had broken an unwritten rule. There's a similar feeling in the Yorkshire Grey. People come in to work, chew over ideas, and discuss business. It's more like a local than your average West End pub, where a load of tourists will suddenly arrive. It's tucked away and just that little bit hard to find. Studio YG1, for those in the know.

It's a far cry from the days of the legendary drinking clubs of Soho. These establishments flourished before 24-hour drinking laws and I suppose the change in the legislation has put paid to them. When the pubs closed at 3 p.m. and you still fancied a drink, you'd head off to one of these places, almost invariably located in a basement. They were suitably dingy places, overpriced, and with candles stuffed into bottles to provide basic lighting. It was all seen to be very raffish and rakish back then but I enjoyed it. There was a particular club in Shaftesbury Avenue called Gerry's which was run by Gerald Campion, the actor who played Billy Bunter in the 1950s BBC TV series. Gerry's was a very popular place in its heyday, offering actors, sporting stars, writers and journalists a late drink and the chance to let their hair down. With only a small brass plate screwed to the wall, it wasn't an easy place to find but once you were there, it could go on well into the night. More often than not, you'll be pleased to hear, I left at a reasonable hour to get the train back home. As a result, I wasn't there on the night that Mornington Crescent was invented.

'I'm Sorry I Haven't A Clue'[7] fans will know what I'm talking about, but for the uninitiated, this is a game in which the rules take precedence over the actual game itself. I think it's probably easier if you tune in to the show to find out more.[8] Anyway, the legend goes that there were three or four people there, including Pat Johns, the TV director. They were talking away when a man sat down next to them, completely uninvited. They were too polite to ask him to leave, but it became clear that he wasn't going to be frozen out easily. So, when he disappeared to the gents, one of them suggested that they invent a game to discourage their interloper. Someone then had the idea of basing it on Tube stations and a brief but intense discussion followed. Finally, Mornington Crescent was decided on as the winning hand. To his surprise, the man returned to find that a very serious game had begun in his absence. Locations like Goodge Street and Oxford Circus were shouted out and greeted by things like 'lovely move!' and 'ooh, nice one!' Each time the man attempted to join in, he was met with disapproving looks. They told him that, since he was a novice, he would need the rules explained to him. Needless to say, the rules became more and more complex and bizarre as the game progressed.

And that's the definitive version of how Mornington Crescent started. Or at least that's what I was told by a man who claimed to be there. In a drinking club. In 1970. At four o'clock in the morning. And who am I to doubt it?

---

7 Hereafter to be known simply as 'Clue'.
8 BBC Radio 4 Mondays 6.30 p.m. and the live show coming to a theatre near you soon.

The Irresistible Rise of Chairman Humph

I used to look at these pictures of trumpeters pointing their instrument to the ceiling. Stunning pictures, but if you play the trumpet and point it upwards, all the spit comes back into your mouth.

HUMPHREY RICHARD ADEANE LYTTELTON or

HUMPH for short

A few years ago, I went into hospital to have my leaking aorta repaired. It was a worrying time, but I'm pleased to say that I made a full recovery thanks to my surgeon, Sir Magdi Yacoub.[1] It had all started after a check-up with my GP, Alan Byers. He told me that he'd heard a flutter in my chest, and for safety's sake was going to send me to nearby Harefield Hospital. They gave me a check-over and asked me if I wanted to see my heart on the ultrasound machine. 'Only if it's a moving picture,' I replied. Then they delivered the bad news about my aorta.

Thankfully, it was minimal at that stage and it didn't need a repair. However, after three years of clear checks (and a certain amount of regrettable complacency), I was told that I finally needed an operation. It took place on 10 September 2001, and when I woke up full of drugs the

---

1 See – I can even name-drop surgeons!

following day, I thought I was hallucinating. The TV was showing pictures of planes crashing into tall buildings and I thought I was watching a Bruce Willis film. Terry, who was at my bedside, explained what had been happening in New York and apparently, I cried. Although I can't remember any of it.

I related my experiences to Humphrey Lyttelton just before he went in to have an aortic aneurysm repaired. 'Don't worry,' I told him, 'Sir Magdi Yacoub said it's only plumbing.[2] You'll be fine.' I had no reason to think otherwise. Humph was Humph. He had always been a resilient, hard-working professional. He proved this by performing with his band and recording with us, right up to the time he went into hospital. Even then, he postponed the operation for as long as he could, because he wanted to fulfil his obligation to the touring version of our show. However, there were voices of concern for Humph and what he might have to face in hospital. Graeme Garden had trained as a doctor before the Cambridge Footlights took his career in a different direction. 'I'm worried about Humph,' he told me quietly one afternoon during a break in rehearsals. 'I think the anaesthetic will knock him sideways, never mind the operation.' Such was Humph's energy; it was easy to overlook the fact that he was eighty-six. I felt fortunate that I'd had my aorta repaired at sixty-six.

---

2 It's not that often you get to name-drop a knighted Professor of Cardiothoracic Surgery, so I thought I'd take the opportunity to do it twice. Incidentally, I once worked with Larry Adler, the virtuoso harmonica player, and if you think I'm a name dropper he was just amazing. A friend of mine, Roger Kitter, said he went into Bloom's restaurant in London with Larry, and Larry looked round and said, 'I came in here forty years ago with Cole Porter.' The man behind the counter said, 'We're serving as fast as we can, sir.'

I went to visit him in hospital before the operation and was cheered to discover that he was still the same witty, urbane man I'd first met outside Leeds town hall in 1955. He was thirty-four and already a star and I was the singer in a Leeds University jazz band busking on the town hall steps. He and his band were playing a show that night, and he spotted our band while he stretched his legs before the gig.

'Humphrey Lyttelton,' he said, stretching out his hand with typical courtesy.

'I know,' I replied, somewhat star-struck.

'I heard you singing with the band,' he said.

I preened myself, flattered that he'd taken notice.

'It wasn't difficult, you're quite loud.'

Back then, he was sporting the goatee beard and side-burns that all fashionable young jazzers seemed to have at the time. In hospital, he was dressed in a rather unflattering nightshirt and socks, but the sense of humour was the same. We laughed and talked for the best part of an hour. He told me about his own experiences with the ultrasound. When the nurse asked him if he wanted to see it, he said, 'No thank you. I never watch daytime television.' He was in such good form that I could've stayed all day. As I left, I was full of optimism. 'There's nothing wrong with him,' I thought, 'he's in great shape.' Apparently, he said to someone before the operation, 'If all goes well, this year's drama will be next year's anecdote.'

Humph was an old school gentleman in many ways, but he also defied the expectations of his class and background. The Lytteltons were an aristocratic English family and his dad was the second son of Viscount Cobham and a house-master at Eton. So, not only did Humph attend the school but he was actually born there as well. He could easily have become a judge or a gentleman farmer, and the world would've been denied a great trumpeter. However, an early love for Louis Armstrong intervened and set Humph off in a different direction. There was another influence, too. Just after leaving school, and for reasons that I'm still not sure of to this day, Humph went to south Wales, where he spent time among steelworkers. This would have been in the tur-bulent years of the late 1930s, just before the Second World War, and the experience changed Humph for life. His upbringing and education at Eton were placed in sharp contrast to the harsh lives of these people. From that moment on, Humph became a committed left-winger. His com-mitment today might have attracted the rather derogatory term 'champagne socialism', but Humph was very firm in his views and they never wavered. Neither did his membership of the Labour Party.

Nonetheless, Humph took up a commission with the Grenadier Guards in 1941 and saw action across Europe. The story goes that he was on the front line when the Allies invaded Italy, coming ashore at Salerno with a pistol in one hand and a trumpet in the other. Another war-related story claimed that he played his trumpet outside the gates of Buckingham Palace, amidst mass celebrations on VE night. This particular musical tale turned out to have an interesting coda. Humph had told that story for years, but as time went by, he began to have doubts about the veracity of it. Like many stories, he wondered whether a grain of truth had grown into something bigger. Two members of his band, similarly intrigued about the truth of the story, dug into the BBC archives and by a stroke of luck found a recording of the event. They heard the broadcaster Howard Marshall talking over the sound of a trumpet playing 'Roll Out the Barrel'. They agreed the trumpet was unmistakeably Humph's, and he was moved and delighted when a CD of the broadcast was given to him as a present.

After the war, he went to Camberwell Art College and then joined the *Daily Mail* as a cartoonist, working on the Flook strip. For a while, fellow jazz musician George Melly provided the words for the cartoon and the two became good friends. A few years later Humph was asked to write a restaurant column. George also wrote restaurant reviews, so Humph sought his opinion.

'George, I don't know what I'm talking about,' he confided.

'Carry on writing it,' said George. 'By the time they've realised you don't know what you're talking about, you will know what you're talking about.'

However, like George, Jazz was Humph's abiding passion and he was already beginning to gather around him musicians that would form the backbone of the trad jazz revival of the early 1950s. Although Humph's life had taken this rather dramatic departure from his background, his family were completely supportive of the leftie jazzer in their midst. When I first came down to London, I used to bump into Humph at places like the 100 Club and Ronnie Scott's. We knew each other to say hello, but that was about as far as our friendship got. Until 1972 that is, and the first series of 'Clue'.

It was either David Hatch or Humphrey Barclay, the two producers involved in the planning of the first series, who decided it would be a good idea to put Humph in the role of chairman. Humph made the role all his own and quickly evolved the courteous, yet slightly irritated tone that made him such a favourite with the audience. He was the toff in the room of oiks, the head teacher among the schoolboys, the urbane man in close proximity to the idiots. He sounded like he just wanted to get the whole thing over and go home. Although Humph was a witty man in his own right, the introduction of writer Iain Pattinson crystallised the chairman's role into something quite brilliant. Iain worked in the double entendres that have become a key feature of the show and Humph delivered them with as much innocence, naivety and ennui as he could feign. He loved delivering such 'blue chip filth'.[3] He also loved it when you took liberties with him. I would sometimes walk off in mock outrage at something he'd said[4] and whenever I shouted things at him, he would often turn to me and say, 'And you are?'

Humph was a very down-to-earth man, without a hint of snobbery. There are many bandleaders who are respected, many that are liked and many that aren't liked by their bands. However, there are very few, like Humph, that are loved. His band knew they were good and audiences respected them hugely, but people often came to hear Humph speak as much

---

3 Humph's phrase. q.v. p.30.
4 Humph spoke at an *Oldie* lunch and as he talked he kept looking at me in a strange way. 'Where were you?' he demanded afterwards. 'What do you mean? I was sitting here, listening to you.' 'No,' he said, looking slightly exasperated, 'where were you? I kept expecting you to interrupt me or heckle or something. I was hoping for a sparring partner.'

as they did the band play. One night I saw him and his band on good form in Pinner, which is not too far from where I live.

'Oh, the memories this place brings back,' he said between songs. 'I was playing my trumpet when a butterfly flew from the side of the stage and landed on it. Such a touching moment. I'm getting rather emotional just talking about it.

'Then it fluttered away and burned to death on that lamp just there!'

I was always amazed by Humph's energy after gigs, particularly his insistence on getting out there among the fans to talk, shake hands and sign CDs. He'd almost always pull a box of CDs from his car and set up a desk and chair so he could sign them after the gig. He was very generous with his time, and one of the recipients of his generosity was my own grandson, Evan. He was about eight and was studying the trumpet, so we took him to see Humph's band, clutching his trumpet manual. This old man playing the trumpet fascinated Evan,[5] so we took him backstage.

'Good evening Evan,' Humph beamed. 'How nice of you to come and see me. May I sign your trumpet book?'

The book was produced, and as Humph took out his pen, someone connected with the show came up to talk to him.

'Excuse me,' he said, politely dismissing the person, 'I'm talking.'

Then he drew a lovely picture of a trumpeter and inscribed it:

---

[5] So much so that although he was bursting for a pee he hung on until the end so that he wouldn't miss any of it.

'To Evan, from one trumpeter to another.'

Now, I know it was my grandson, but I've seen Humph do this sort of thing many, many times with members of the public. He was never anything less than polite and courteous. If someone was irritating him, he was never rude, he just treated them as if they were invisible and tuned them out.

He was also an exceptionally private man, and this extended to those he counted as friends. Not one of us ever set foot in his house or even knew his phone number. If you needed to contact him, you had to ring his agent and she would get him to ring you. He kept his private life intensely private, and if his number was ever leaked, he changed it. I once accepted an award on his behalf at an awards ceremony at the Theatre Royal Drury Lane. He told me he would collect it from my house, so I lugged this great heavy glass affair home to Hatch End and waited for the doorbell to ring. At the appointed hour, Humph stood there on the doorstep.

'Come on in,' I said, expecting him to follow.

'No thanks,' he said, still standing at the door.

'Oh come on,' I said, 'just for a second while I go and get it.'

'No thanks,' he repeated politely, 'I'll just wait here.'

I brought the award to the door. He thanked me very kindly, got into his car and drove away. It was typical of the man. Family was one world, work was another and never the twain met, or at least never impinged on each other.

I've heard people say that towards the end of his life, Humph's voice became softer. I never noticed that until

I compared some of the recordings of 'Clue' on Radio 7. He was a little frailer in some of the later ones, but then there aren't many eighty-six-year-olds who don't have some frailties. The voice is softer, but the delivery is still there. It was the same with his trumpet playing. The 'lip' stayed until the end but his playing was more economical and didn't blast as much as it used to do.

After Humph's aorta operation, I had a call from his son Steve asking me to come to Barnet Hospital. I was driven up there and when I eventually saw Humph, he was on a dialysis machine and with wires and tubes everywhere. It distressed me. His system was all but broken down, and I didn't recognise the old man on the bed. Members of his band, as well as his family, were up there and people were drifting in and out of the ward in shifts. His eyes were closed, and it was very difficult to tell if anything was going on under the lids. I leaned over the bed, determined not to go all mushy on him. They say the hearing is the last thing to go and I wanted to honour him by behaving as normally as I could.

'I'm a busy man and this is all very inconvenient. Look at you, like Lord Muck, surrounded by all these nurses.'

A little later, I left his bedside and went home. At 7 p.m., I couldn't wait any longer, so I rang Sue, his manager, for a progress report. 'It's weird for you to ring just now, Baz. Humph went two minutes ago.'

After the funeral, we were told that we were being invited back to his house near Barnet and because none of us had ever been there, it became something of a talking point. When we got there, it appeared that the house had no windows on the outside. It was only when we got inside, that

we realised they all faced inwards to a courtyard garden.[6]
Very Humph.

Humph died on 25 April 2008 and it's still not sunk in yet.
His passing left a huge gap in many lives. Even now, when
I see or hear something I know he'd like, I have to stop myself
from thinking that I can tell him about it later. There hasn't
been an official memorial service yet, but there was a kind of
unofficial gathering a month after his death at the Bull's
Head Pub in Barnes by the Thames. Needless to say, the
pub was packed. Humph and his band had gigged there
religiously every month when they first started out, and
regularly after that. Ronnie Hughes played trumpet in
Humph's place and I was very touched to be invited to
sing. Ronnie was very nervous about it, but the crowd were
wonderful and hugely supportive. Ronnie played a blinder.
He's eighty-two.

Then it was my turn to go on. I knew what I would be
singing. For years Humph had teased me that I would sing
the old standard 'Dr Jazz' with his band before I died. It
became a kind of running joke. So, that night I cleared my
throat and stepped up to the mic to give it my all for the
band, for the audience and for Humph.

His final sign-off on 'Clue' was:

'And so, as the loose-bowelled pigeon of time swoops low
over the unsuspecting tourist of destiny, and the flatulent

---

6 I stood in that garden, nattering away as usual, when I heard a voice say, 'Hello
Barry.' Some feet away, his back turned, was Wally Fawkes, the great cartoonist and
clarinet player who had also worked on the Flook cartoon strip and had played with
Humph many times. Wally can hardly see now, but his hearing is very acute, as
I noticed that afternoon.

skunk of fate wanders into the air-conditioning system of eternity, I notice it's the end of the show.'

Thanks, Humph. You were one of my oldest friends. I miss you dearly.

Ode to Humph

As the trumpeter of eternity sits on the mute of fate
Today we join and celebrate
And sing in praise of peerless Humph
Looking at this sheet of bumf
I realise there's only one rhyme for Humph
But onward – thirty-six years of fun and laughter
1972, 'Clue' was born, I joined soon after
And happily joined in
And memories dawn – I think I win
The hindsight saga – saints alive!
I met him in 1955
A meeting I could never have planned
He was in Leeds, fronting his band
We talked and I recall his wit
Bless him, he said he remembered it
Since then he'd been our adjudicator
Tolerating 'we're going for a walk later'
One of a kind and standing tall
The thinking woman's Kenny Ball
The epitome of his ilk
He's even been compared to Nat Gonella
The gentlest, sweetest natured of men

Saying after each series, 'Never again'
No other chairman can compare
Well, Nicholas ... this is a joke I swear
Turning up, like our own bad penny
Dispelling our blues, if we had any
Thank you for the friendship and fun
I raise my glass – oh, just the one
Cheers, Humph

'I'm Sorry I Haven't a Clue' (about a new series)

Humph's death inevitably called into question the future of 'Clue'. The show had survived a tragedy before, with the death of Willie Rushton in 1996. Will was very much missed, but somehow we'd carried on with a series of special guests. Following Humph's passing, the recording of the next series was postponed indefinitely, and none of us really had any idea what might happen next. After all, Humph once said, 'If I go under a bus, I want no displays of loyalty.' He meant it. Only Humph could be Humph, and it seemed pointless to expect anyone else to try and carry on in his unique vein. If the show had ended, then I would have been very sad but accepted that thirty-seven years is quite an achievement for a radio show.

However, the BBC was flooded with emails, making it difficult to ignore the public's appetite for a new recording. If, in recent years, 'Clue' has established itself as something of a cult show, then it is in no small part down to the work of producer Jon Naismith. He has kept the show fresh with a much more flexible format and, as a result, our audience figures had grown. Jon is the best producer we've ever had, and it's mainly down to the fact that he won't leave the show alone. He prods it and pokes it all the time, making sure that it is fluid and not becoming set in its ways. I think it is all the stronger for it. Amazingly, Jon said that he felt nervous at the beginning, because we'd all been in the show for a long time. As a result, he wanted plenty of input from the start and we respected that. Conversely, we welcomed his suggestions and his way of looking at things differently. If there is one defining moment of his tenure it was his decision to take the show on the road and into regional theatres. It's noticeable that this formula has since been copied by other shows.

We've had many guest panellists including Paul Merton, Sandi Toksvig, Ross Noble, Jeremy Hardy, Tony Hawks, Denise Coffey, Bill Bailey, Phill Jupitus and the late Linda Smith[7] but we've never had a guest chairman. We wondered whether any one of them would want to commit to the chairman's role full-time. One thing was for certain, none of the regular panellists wanted to take over the job. The suggestion was made, on the basis that one of us would be most comfortable with the move over, but quickly dismissed. The role of panellist is very different to that of chairman. Personally, I've done quite a bit of chairmanship and I'd much rather be a panellist.

We also had some very left-field suggestions for the role,

---

7 I've included the names of several female panellists because whilst we've never intended it to be a male dominated show, for some reason we've had difficulty in booking female guests. I have no answer to why this is the case, save only to say that I find it a shame.

one of the most memorable being the actor Michael Gambon.[8] He's a great actor and a real maverick, and I think he would be an excellent addition for a later series. However, for the first series, we felt that sticking to 'Clue's' extended family was the best way forward. After some deliberation, it was announced in February 2009 that Stephen Fry, Jack Dee and Rob Brydon would host two shows each, to be recorded in April, May and June 2009.

We knew Stephen and Jack from their appearances as panellists, and Rob holds the rare distinction of being the only person, other than Humph and myself,[9] to have been chairman. When Humph was in hospital, Rob stepped into the role for the last date of the live stage tour in 2008. Bournemouth Conference Centre was packed, and what Jon Naismith hadn't told us was that Humph had recorded a message especially for the evening. Rob Brydon was about to begin, when suddenly we heard the following:

'Sorry I can't be with you tonight, I'm in hospital. Oh, I wish I'd thought of this earlier. Give a big welcome to Rob Brydon.'

Rob described his role as not trying to fill Humph's shoes but just taking over the job, which I think was an immaculate description. Sharing the job between the three of them made

---

8 Some years ago, there was a play being recorded for Yorkshire Television and the great old comedian called Billy Russell, who'd become a character actor, was in it. Michael Gambon was also in the cast. They sat round the table to read the script while having coffee and Billy Russell went very quiet. And he'd passed over. There was a terrible drama, and the director sent the cast to the bar. An actor called Charles Lamb was deputed to come up to London very quickly to replace Billy. Eventually they all reassembled. The director said, 'It was a terrible occurrence but we all have to get on and carry on so let's start.' Gambon said, 'A terrific judge of a script, Billy.'
9 I arrived at the start of the second series and did a couple of recordings when Humph was away.

sense, because they're all so different and this gave the series balance. We were also keen to get the show back on the air before any further speculation grew about a permanent replacement for Humph.

There had been some debate as to whether we do the stage tour[10] before the recording of a new series but Jon said it was more important for us to be on the radio first. After all, that's where 'Clue' began in 1972, and that's where most people still come across it.

So, we all gathered at Her Majesty's Theatre in London on 26 April of this year[11] for the first two recordings of the show without Humph. Giving us 'silly things to do' on this occasion was Stephen Fry. Jon came out before the show to explain that the whole evening was dedicated to Humph's memory. Then we told a few of Humph's favourite jokes and the recording got under way, with Victoria Wood occupying the guest panellist's chair. Jon had been asking her to come on the show for about nine years and, although she was a fan, she declined. She'd thought there was 'too much pissing about'. Anyway, his powers of persuasion finally worked and I'm pleased to say that the shows went down well. I think this was mainly because we tried to keep as much continuity as possible. There were appearances from our scorers Samantha and Sven and Hamish and Dougal turned up in Sound Charades. Stephen ably monitored Mornington Crescent for the first time and gave the impression that he'd been doing it for years. He also didn't mind a bit of ribbing about his

---

10 See below.
11 As of writing, 2009. But for tax purposes, 1987.

Twitter habit.[12] We soon realised that the atmosphere was one of love and memories, not solemn mourning. I like to think that Humph was in the wings that night, watching, listening and perhaps modestly approving.

As I write, it's the middle of May and we're about to record the other shows in Southampton and Newcastle, with Jack and Rob. The current show is starting to feel like an homage to Humph, which I like. It also genuinely feels like a new beginning for 'Clue', and while it's still early days, the support for it is very heartening. No one could ever occupy Humph's territory in the history 'Clue', and I don't think any of our new chairmen would want to. However, the reality is that the show goes on, and it's still falling apart as gracefully and noisily as ever. Like I said, it's been thirty-seven years since we started and if it all ended tomorrow we'd have no cause to complain.

Although we'd still complain.

'Clue' Live!

The first live tour of the show last year was a great success. Initially, we had all these visual ideas for the show but Jon wanted us to keep the staging as true to the radio recordings as possible. He pointed out that those who'd been to a 'Clue' recording knew what they were coming to see and those who hadn't might be intrigued to see what a recording is like. At first we thought it might be too plain, but actually it's worked out very well. However, we do make some concessions to the stage. For example, songs are sung at the front under a spotlight. The whole thing is really a parade of 'Clue's' 'greatest hits' and therefore more heavily scripted than a recording.

I remember, years ago, seeing the Monty Python stage show in London and having to ask the man next to me to be quiet, because he was reciting the Parrot Sketch well ahead of the performers. With 'Clue', we haven't yet got to the stage where people come in silly hats or dressed as characters from the show, but there's certainly a jolly club atmosphere. The roar that goes up when Mornington Crescent is announced could knock you off your chair. The audiences are now so large that you don't spot the familiar faces like you used to do when we were recording in small venues like the Paris Cinema.[1] Now we tour in theatres and often they're

---

1 What has 47 legs and 33 teeth? The front row at the Paris Theatre.

pleased to see you because you've made the effort to come to their town. At the Lowry Centre in Manchester, they booked us for a matinee and an evening performance of the stage show, and 1,400 people turned up for each show. We played in front of 3,500 at the Hammersmith Apollo, and while you might think that such a large venue and a big crowd might take away some of the atmosphere, the opposite seems to be true. In fact, we broke a world record there for the number of people playing kazoos at the same time.[2]

The late Miles Kington wrote a piece about 'Clue', in which he said that shows like this become soap operas. People sometimes ask me who came up with the idea for this or that part of the show, but it's hard to answer definitively because themes and running jokes have simply evolved over the years. You can't actually remember how the stock characters or situations evolved, but somehow they did. And everybody plays a role – old Cryer with his jokes, the dry Graeme Garden, Tim Brooke-Taylor the jolly audience man and, until last year, the great Lyttelton as the bewildered, bored patrician. So it's like acting in a sense, although I've never been conscious of playing a role as such – perhaps you just do it without thinking. And if you're lucky this all falls into place, but as has often been said about 'Clue', the best moments are when it is falling apart or at least on the verge of it. So, the new series would be followed by a live tour, with Jack Dee signed up for the duration.[3]

---

2 Jon found out that the record was 2,000, so we put a kazoo on every seat and we got the whole crowd to play at the same time. I have a lovely picture of Humphrey Lyttelton, the great jazz trumpeter, with a kazoo between his lips.
3 Which you'll have hopefully enjoyed by now. Weren't we good? The duration, Wayne, is a reference to the length of the Second World War.

The Birth of 'Hamish & Dougal'

The expert's expert on 'Give Us a Clue', was Lionel Blair. Who can ever forget opposing team captain Una Stubbs sitting open mouthed as he tried to pull off *Twelve Angry Men* in under two minutes.

HUMPHREY LYTTELTON,[4] *York, 15 November 1999*

If I had a favourite round, it would have to be Sound Charades. By way of explaining it to the uninitiated, it's probably best that I quote Humph again, who said:

'In the original (charades), the players were not allowed to speak, resulting in much hilarity. Our version differs subtly in two ways.'

The two Scottish characters, Hamish and Dougal, evolved out of Sound Charades, along with their catchphrase, 'You'll have had your tea.'[5] At first, the two characters weren't called anything at all, but as time went on we decided to give them proper names and characters. Jon Naismith was always very keen on Hamish and Dougal and we were delighted when he suggested a spin-off. Graeme and I wrote and recorded a series which was first broadcast at the end of 2002. It featured Alison Steadman as Mrs Naughtie, the housekeeper, and Jeremy Hardy as the local laird. The episodes were only 15 minutes long, but were a real joy to write and perform. We did wonder how the show might go down in Scotland, but

---

4 Via Iain Pattinson.
5 The repetition of which brings out groans from Tim.

Graeme has always maintained that we're sending up the stereotype of the kilted man that the Scots are already fed up with. Sure enough, the general reaction north of the border has been encouraging. In fact in 2004, we did a Hogmanay special with guest appearances from James Naughtie (the 'Today' programme presenter, who appeared as Mrs Naughtie's son) and Sandi Toksvig, along with Humph, Tim and Colin Sell.

The 'Hamish & Dougal' series has lots of sound effects and it's full of the kind of jokes that you can only do on the radio. One of my favourite bits is when Hamish and Dougal are walking back from 'the big hoose' and Graeme says:

> 'Well, here's my front door, I don't know what it's doing lying in the middle of the road.'

Then we hearing him open it, before saying goodnight. It's pure radio and couldn't work anywhere else.[6]

---

6 Apart than as a book, obviously. *The Doings of Hamish and Dougal: You'll Have Had Your Tea?* by Barry Cryer & Graeme Garden, Preface Publishing (1998).

Interval [1]

And now, the weather . . . [2]

Followed by

A Partly Political Broadcast

Bill and Hillary Clinton once had George W. and Laura
Bush over to dinner. And after the meal, Dubya said, 'I have
to take a leak, Bill.' So Bill showed him where to go. When
George was finished, he came back and said, 'Hey Bill, real
class, a gold toilet.' After George and Laura had gone home,
Hillary turned to Bill and said, 'There you go, Bill, another
one's pissed in your saxophone.'

I don't deal in political jokes. They tend to get elected. If
I do, I'm reminded of the time we did 'Clue' at the Theatre
Royal in Brighton, not long after the bombing.[3] We recorded
two shows, back to back, and in the interval, we were chatting

---

[1] This is the same interval as used for the RSC's recent production of *King Lear*.
Drink up, the second half's about to start.
[2] Overcast until noon. Brightening up later.
[3] Willie Rushton and I encountered an old man at Macclesfield railway station the
morning after the Brighton bombing. Everyone was in shock but this man breezed
on to the platform, 'Mornin' lads,' he said, 'what a day, eh? That bomb in Brighton,
a train crash in London and I tripped over the dog this morning and my bitten foot's
come up like a balloon. It's true – these things come in threes!'

with the audience and cracking jokes. Suddenly there was an almighty thunderclap and Humph said, 'Oh God, it brings back memories of the Grand Hotel!' Not to be outdone, I added, 'Yes, do you remember, we all went down to breakfast together?' There was something of an uneasy reaction from some of the audience and I wasn't sure whether I'd drawn the line correctly on that one. So, welcome to Part Three in my series of lectures on Taste, Swearing and Politics in Comedy: Why I know everything.[4]

Political humour is a strange beast. Generally, I think politicians are legitimate targets for fun but it's often a case of choosing the right time. Jo Brand got into hot water recently for her comments about Lady Thatcher. 'Is that a device for removing pubic hair?' she joked on BBC's 'QI'. Several senior Tories demanded an apology from her and criticised the BBC for their left-wing bias. Personally, I thought it was just a very funny joke. It wasn't really anything to do with politics. It was more of a pun, but some objected because she was picking on an old woman who had long since left office. However, you can't help thinking that some of those senior Tories were out to even the score, after Jo had 'outed' Carol Thatcher for her views on French tennis players.

I'm not a card-carrying member of any political party and I never have been. 'Soft centre' is how Alan Bennett once described himself politically, and perhaps that applies to me too. Privately, I don't mind very much who people are, as long as they're interesting. However, I know that as a per-

---

4 In which Soames and Irene board the helicopter gunship to look for Colonel Kurtz.

former I have to be aware that allegiances do run deep in this country. I once met an old Yorkshireman who had Harold Macmillan as his MP. I asked him what Macmillan was like.

'He was bloody good. Knew exactly what was going on round here. A good MP.'

'Did you vote for him?' I asked.

'Vote for him? No. Labour all my life.'

Recalling Macmillan makes me realise just how much has changed in the political landscape since I grew up.[5] We've finally got rid of that troublesome Lord North for one. One thing you could say about those old patrician Tories was that they'd been brought up with an ethos of public service. They would never have accepted a bung in a brown envelope.[6] That generation had been through two wars that had decimated every stratum of society and those left behind understood what real hardship meant. The only two I can think of that are still active from that period are Tony Benn and Denis Healey. They're both worth listening to. Amazingly, Tony Benn has even become something of a national treasure. It's hard to believe, thinking back to the way he was demonised all those years ago and I wonder what those who called him 'Loony Benn' think now. Firebrands are made slightly differently these days.

I once hosted an *Oldie* lunch in the absence of Richard Ingrams. That particular day I'd been with George Galloway, the firebrand rebel MP. We were in Harrogate, which is not natural territory for George, and indeed, the audience was

---

5 Some say I haven't yet.
6 It would've been white.

populated by a large number of gentlemen in blazers and cravats and ladies sporting blue rinses.

I stood up to introduce him.

'Fasten your seatbelts,' I said, 'it's George Galloway.'

George is nothing if not a showman, and he kicked off with three or four very good jokes, instantly making the audience laugh. I don't know why, but I'm always interested in the mavericks, the loose cannons, the rebels and the black sheep. George held an instant attraction for me too. I admired his style, but I didn't want to let the great and good of Harrogate off with nothing more than just entertainment. 'Come on, George,' I thought, 'change gear.'

Sure enough, he commenced a tirade about the Iraq war, condemning George W. Bush and Tony Blair, and he didn't stop until he was almost out of breath. At the end of his speech, the audience practically gave him a standing ovation. He'd superbly won round what might have been a very hostile crowd. After the lunch, he and I were talking about Tony Blair, and George remarked on how different he looked since he first appeared as the young, fresh-faced Prime Minister in 1997.

'We might see a disintegration as time goes on,' I said, 'what with the stress and the strain and the opposition he's facing. His face might begin to look like a fire in a waxworks.'

George beamed. 'Can I have that?' he asked.

I remember Ken Livingstone arriving to speak at a Lord's Taverners lunch years ago, in the days when he was 'Red Ken'. There was much muttering among the older members about the 'awful' Livingstone, but of course he charmed the flannels off them. I remember him remarking and pointing to his head, 'can you see where the horns were?' He made them laugh and talked about cricket and sports facilities for young people.

Another rebel I had the pleasure of meeting was Tam Dalyell, the now-former Labour MP who pursued Margaret Thatcher endlessly about the torpedoing of the *General Belgrano* ship during the Falklands War. I had a sneaking regard for him because he was like a dog with a bone over the issue and wouldn't let it go. We shook hands at the lunch and I said,

'You're a pain in the arse, aren't you?'

'Yes,' he said, smiling broadly.

In television, that patrician officer-generation, typified by Macmillan, was particularly in evidence during the 1960s and 1970s, and it was interesting to watch how they worked alongside natural showmen like Bill Cotton and Lew Grade. At the BBC we used to call them the 'blazerati' and, generally, they were liked and respected, even if they did represent another generation. It's a bit like George Martin and the Beatles. Their backgrounds couldn't have been more different yet they saw things in one another that they liked and, more importantly, that they needed to work on to make the band a success. The Beatles were talented but George Martin showed them how to use a studio and produce a record. There he was, in his suit and tie, telling these young Scousers how it should sound and they respected him for it. Unfortunately, the creative tension that was created when the toffs and the proles worked together in those days just doesn't seem to be there any more.

This is partly because television today reflects the obsession with consensus that is now so prevalent in politics. The bottom line now is money and budgets. It's a familiar complaint, but the suits do seem to have taken over. These are often people who've never made or written a TV programme in their lives. Their output is softly middle-class; nice to watch but without much to say for itself. Looking back, Monty Python was full of authority figures; the doctors, lawyers, ministry officials and public-school teachers that the Pythons might've become. They reacted against the expectations they'd grown up with and expressed it in their shows. Now I see so much self-analysis and self-doubt among younger entertainers and I worry about them. You hear about successful people who are full of terrible self-loathing and seem to want to do anything other than the thing they're doing. Perhaps a lot of entertainers, particularly comedians, have always been this way, but some people feel it's now a duty to be a broken-hearted clown.

What has also changed noticeably since I started is the number of comedians who've been to university. Not many of the comics I worked with had been through further education. Most had left school early and had gone straight into variety shows or had come up through working men's clubs. That might explain why a fair few of them were right wing. Bernard Manning is a classic example. He grew up in the school of hard knocks and although he didn't touch on politics, his place on the political spectrum was obvious when you looked at his attitudes to race and gender. Although this may sound controversial, he was technically a good comedian. As Alexei Sayle once observed,

'He's a good comic with a lamentable act.'

Unfortunately, in the later stages of his life, he became overtly offensive. Our paths crossed quite a few times and I never had a problem with Bernard. If I was on my feet speaking and he was in the audience, he never heckled like he did to others. I suppose I was lucky.

The recent generation of comics, who've come through the university system, have created a political climate where the starting point seems to be that you have to be left of centre. There are a few comics out there who play the right-wing toff, but they largely seem to be doing it as an ironic joke. That's a tradition that's always been there. The likes of Will Hay and George Robey playing upper-class twits springs to mind. I think it would be very refreshing to watch a funny genuinely right-wing comedian today.[7] It would give some balance to the scene.

That's not to say that left-wing comedians dominate without merit. Mark Thomas is superb. He's this country's answer to Michael Moore. Some people are surprised when they find out that he's a friend of mine. We're poles apart, Mark and I. He's an angry polemicist and I'm a gag teller. We did two nights at the Red Rose Club in Seven Sisters Road in London. He was to be the firebrand opening comedian for a similarly militant audience and I started to feel my nerve going just before the show started. My hands were shaking and my mouth was dry.

---

7 Boris Johnson doesn't count.

'Mark, I'm not right for this,' I said.

'Don't worry,' he said, patting my shoulder, 'I'll introduce you. It'll be OK.'

He then went on and did twenty-five minutes of searing political comedy and I stood in the wings losing the will to live.

Then Mark ended his act by saying, 'There are two kings in the world. One died on the lavatory in Memphis, the other is here tonight. Give it up for Barry Cryer!'

Well, at that moment I nearly jumped out of the window and ran all the way back to Hatch End but somehow I stepped on to the stage and decided to do my act as usual. I suppose I felt there was no point doing otherwise. As I walked on, a young girl sitting in the front row went 'ah', as if her granddad had just appeared. It turned out to be a great night and I really enjoyed it. Afterwards Mark confronted me,

'You bugger, Baz, I couldn't get an "ah" if I tried.'

'You've just got to get older, Mark,' I said.

Jeremy Hardy[8] is another comedian who's also a very committed political activist. However, although he's very serious about it, he can take the piss out of himself. He explains to his audiences that he is a 'middle-class Marxist'. I once went to see him at the Cochrane Theatre in London on the same day as the police had been demonstrating about low pay in front of the House of Commons.

---

8 Jeremy Hardy once had a drunken heckler who could hardly make sense. Three or four times this man tried to heckle and Jeremy put him down each time. On the fifth occasion, Jeremy looked at him and said camply, 'Simon, it's over.'

'They should've had miners on horseback controlling them,' Jeremy said.

He also said that if you want to stay out of trouble at a demo, you shouldn't stand next to an anarchist. He once said,

'It's all right for you with your dog on a string, my daughter's got a violin lesson in two hours.'

The closest I've ever got to political activism was when I had an attack of the SDPs in the mid 1980s. Roy Jenkins, Shirley Williams, Bamber Gascoigne and I did two meetings for the party in Crosby and Formby, near Liverpool. Shirley had been a Labour MP in the area and her defection to the SDP had caused a lot of resentment. As we walked into one of the meetings, a woman said to me, 'Are you with this lot, Barry?' and when I replied that I was, she spat on me. You don't forget that in a hurry.

The actor Clive Dunn has been a lifelong member of the Labour Party and he told me once about a Workers Revolutionary Party meeting at Wembley Arena some years ago. Clive went along to sing some songs and tell some jokes for Vanessa Redgrave,[9] who was organising.

---

9 I worked with Vanessa Redgrave when she guested on a 'Morecambe & Wise Show' and found her to be delightful. We had a happy time on that particular show as she admired Eric, and Ernie was a very good sport throughout. However, we did hear stories afterwards that she could be difficult when it came to politics. We were told that she'd been doing a Noël Coward play in the West End and had been voted in as the Equity shop steward for the company. Fifteen actors were in the cast and she was voted in by 12 votes to 3. Apparently she'd caused consternation among some of the cast and crew by bringing in copies of the Workers Revolutionary Party newspaper, of which she was a fervent member. Some backstage hands had taken umbrage at this and put a notice on the stage door noticeboard. It read, 'No more milk and papers until further notice.'

In the dressing room he found Spike Milligan[10] clutching a bottle of wine. Clive went on, did his thing and came off to find Spike sitting in the same place, still clutching the bottle of wine. He didn't seem to be contributing to the evening at all. Spike was very environmentally active but I don't think he was a party political man. His humour was far too off the scale to connect with anything topical. Peter Cook was the same. It seems bizarre that someone so strongly associated with the satire boom of the early 1960s was, privately, not really a political animal at all. He enjoyed poking fun at authority, but like Spike, his humour was largely drawn from surreal nonsense, not explicit social comment.

Every joke is a small revolution.[11]

GEORGE ORWELL

People make jokes in the most horrible of situations as a way of transporting themselves from the misery that surrounds

---

10 I remember being on a short-lived chat show on Thames as a guest and when I entered the Green Room, there was Spike, who was booked to appear on the same show. As soon as he saw me he jumped up and splayed himself against the wall saying, 'Cryer's here, take my jokes, don't hurt me!' Spike and Peter Sellers were clones – very mercurial, very one day on, one day off. On a good day you could laugh all day long with Spike and Peter. They would be like children, laughing and clowning all the time and loving life. Then the next day Spike would be staring at the wall wondering, 'How can we bring kids into this world?' You never knew what the score was, and you often had to sniff the wind to find out. Spike rang me out of the blue one evening. 'Cryer,' he said, 'Eric Sykes and I were going to write a script but Eric can't do it. What do you think? Could you do it?' I didn't hesitate to accept but I immediately thought, 'Oh my God I'm going to write with Spike Milligan.' It would either be great or a disaster. Whichever, it was not an opportunity to be missed. Sadly it never happened. I never found out what the idea was as Spike died soon after. One that has to go in the box marked 'If Only'.
11 Although I'd amend that to every good joke is a revolution, and besides, George never played the Theatre Royal, Bilston. Orwell also said that 'A dirty joke is a sort of mental rebellion'. Who knew the old boy was such an expert?

them.[12] As I write, there are probably people in Zimbabwe doing Mugabe jokes whilst looking over their shoulder. In fact, earlier this year, the children's laureate, Michael Rosen, did a superb radio programme about jokes under dictatorships.

One tale occurred during the perestroika period of openness to the West in the former Soviet Union.[13] Back then, the word Russia was regarded as taboo by the KGB. The story goes that a barber was cutting a customer's hair one day and he uttered the dreaded word. He was shopped by one of the customers and hauled in by the KGB.

'You can't use that word,' they said, 'one more, and you'll pay the price.'

He was released and went back to work. A few days later, he was cutting a customer's hair when he used the word again. He was shopped once more by one of the customers and again found himself in front of the KGB.

'We warned you,' they said, 'why are you doing this?'

'Well,' he said, 'every time I mention the word, my customer's hair stands on end.'

Rosen's programme also contained the ultimate in black

---

12 Sandi Toksvig tells the story about travelling in a taxi in Belfast with John McCarthy, who had been held as a hostage for quite some time. And the driver said, 'Mr McCarthy, wouldn't you be happier in the boot?'

13 When Leonid Brezhnev was leader, he decided to make a state visit to Poland. Protocol demanded that he took a present for the Polish leader. He summoned his entourage and said, 'I want a painting of Lenin in Poland.' They went away, came back, and said no such painting existed. Brezhnev demanded they commission a painter. They said a lot had been locked up as dissidents. 'Release one,' said Brezhnev. Cohen the painter appeared before Brezhnev and was given his orders. A few days later, the entourage said that Cohen had finished. Brezhnev asked to see it, and was astonished to see that it was of a couple in bed. Brezhnev said, 'That man is Trotsky. Who is the woman?' 'Mrs Lenin,' Cohen replied. Brezhnev said, 'Where's Lenin?' and Cohen said, 'He's in Poland.'

humour. Jewish prisoners were lined up in a concentration camp and an SS officer told them they would all be hanged that afternoon.

'Great news,' said one, 'they've run out of bullets.'

While on the subject of black humour, I'll conclude with a story of a journalist who went to Jerusalem and visited the Wailing Wall. He saw a very old man praying against the Wall and respectfully waited for him to finish before interviewing him.

'How long have you been praying against the wall?' he asked.

'Over sixty years,' the old man replied.

'What do you pray for?' 'I pray for peace and love and unity between Christians, Jews and Muslims.'

'I see,' said the journalist. 'How does it feel after sixty years?'

'Like talking to a fucking brick wall.'

Touring

Around the end of the 1980s I began to notice that my professional life was becoming a little less busy. The phone didn't ring as often as it used to, and I wasn't spending as much time at the kitchen table, working on scripts. It didn't take long for me to realise that I was approaching a gear change. Luckily for me, a new avenue opened up when Willie Rushton and I were asked to do a gig together for the Spinal Injuries Association. We asked Colin Sell, 'Clue's' resident pianist, to provide the musical accompaniment. We were joined by a brilliant comedian called Pierre Hollins, who used to jump through a newspaper and shout, in a mock French accent, 'Danger is my business.' Christine Pilgrim, who I'd worked with in musicals, came aboard as our singer and Graeme Garden had a funny act with a plastic fruit bat that came out of a box and attached itself to his face. We performed this show for various charities over the course of a year, until Will, ever the entrepreneur, wondered if we might start doing it for money. He titled it *Two Old Farts in the Night* because he felt we couldn't get done under the Trade Description Act.

Will was the rambling, discursive raconteur and I was the joke man. We were totally different, but those differences amounted to a whole and it seemed to work. We came on together at the beginning and the end, but did our own bits in between. The live atmosphere brought me right back to my first outings as a stand-up in Leeds. I loved the thrill of it and working with Will in this way was a dream. We soon recruited my daughter, Jack, and she did the opening number for us. She did a parody of Edith Piaf's 'No Regrets' about giving up smoking called 'No Cigarettes', as the stage filled with smoke.

Around that time, Will's son Toby, an actor, was performing in *The Duchess of Malfi* at a small theatre on the Edinburgh fringe. Will rang the venue and asked the manager, Tomek Borg, if they had a late-night show after the play. As they hadn't, Will asked if they'd like one. Suddenly, I was packing my bags and heading north.

We had a huge amount of fun with the show at Edinburgh, and Will and I did it off and on after that, all over the country. Will was a bit like Ken Dodd,[1] once he was on he was bloody difficult to get off. We played the Harrow Arts Centre which is two minutes' walk from my house, and I remarked that I could quite easily pop home at the interval or, come to think of it, while Will was on.

Will and I once had a booking in Andover. We arrived in the late afternoon to be greeted by the piano tuner. He was blind, as many tuners are, with the compensatory acute hearing, and his guide dog, called Falcon, accompanied him. The man was chatting to us, which was pleasant at first but soon became embarrassing as it became clear he wasn't going to leave us alone. He kept following us around, talking and talking, and we didn't know what to do. He took up residence in our dressing room and we knew that one of us was eventually going to have to ask him to leave as we had a show to do. Suddenly, he picked up the dog's lead and said, 'I hope you have a good show tonight gentlemen.' As he walked out of the door Will said, 'How cruel of them to give you a cat.'

1 If you met Ken Dodd in a bar and got him talking, you'd certainly get your money's worth. Ken is never 'off' and his stamina is unbelievable. He had a hernia operation and the surgeon apparently said, 'I went into the theatre with Mr Dodd and came out four hours later.' The man is eighty-one, and incredible. Some of his best jokes are aimed at accountants and the tax fraud trial he was involved with, and acquitted. 'The Inland Revenue sent a car for me. Luckily I managed to jump out of the way.' There are thousands of them, and he seems to delight in telling them all at one sitting.

My wife and I were on holiday in Jersey once and I saw that Doddy was playing at the Inn on the Park there. When I suggested we go, she said, 'Oh, can't you switch off?' I'll make an exception for Doddy. He's like a force of nature. The band played 'Happiness', his signature tune and on he came. To my surprise, he didn't exactly die but this audience needed a great deal of re-heating. Doddy struggled for 20 minutes or so until he found his rhythm. An hour and three quarters later, those who could stand up, did, and gave him an ovation. I'd never seen anything like it. The man was unstoppable. After the show, we went backstage to wish him well and he invited us back to his hotel. It was a modest establishment, not one of the big flashy ones, and we sat up until three in the morning. I begged him to release us as we wanted to go to bed, but Ken could've talked all night. He also played one of our local theatres, the Beck at Hayes, and I spoke to a neighbour who'd been to see him. 'What was he like?' I asked. 'Well,' said the neighbour, 'it went on for ever. He was wonderful. But in the first half of the show a man shouted out, "Ken, I've booked a taxi for 11" and Doddy said, "you're leaving at the interval?"'

Eric Sykes is still an active performer despite having difficulty with his sight and hearing. He was once telling Doddy about his problems waiting for a cue in the wings, 'I don't know when to go on and you don't know when to come off.'

One Man and his Pianist

I'm a one-man idiot.

EDDIE IZZARD

When we got back from that first trip to Edinburgh I took a phone call from Tristan Taylor, a promoter who had been working with Frankie Howerd. Someone had mentioned to him that I'd recently performed in Scotland with Will and he was wondering if I wanted to do a one-man show. Well, potentially, there was nothing to lose, and after a pint or two in a Marylebone pub, I found myself talked into doing a one-man show. My fears of being up there alone were still present, so immediately I phoned Colin Sell to see if he was up for it. I started to put together what I thought would be a decent two-hour show. There was no theme, just gags, stories, memories, observations, I sing, Colin sings, he tells the odd story and I do some more gags.[1] After input from Colin and a few rehearsals around the piano at my house, we were ready to face an audience. Of three.

We hired a little studio theatre down the road and did the show in front of three friends. They were great, giving us plenty of advice and encouragement, and once we'd

---

[1] Sound familiar?

tweaked it a bit we were ready to inflict ourselves on the paying public.

The first date was at the Brewhouse venue in Taunton. I'd love to give you a detailed account of that first night but unfortunately my usually reliable memory packs up here. All I remember is that the show was two hours long and I went on with a big book that contained the running order. I was so nervous on the night that I was on autopilot, but a lot of people in the bar afterwards said that it was a good baptism. I had to take their word for it and I did, because it was almost twenty years ago and Colin and I have been on the road for a fair portion of the year ever since.

We did the Brighton Comedy Festival quite a few years later. It was at the time when I still had the book of the running order, which was placed on a lectern on the stage. Anyway, the show went down very well and I was feeling rather pleased with myself as I headed towards the bar. As I moved through the throng, up stood a short woman with a fierce expression. It was Joan Littlewood, the legendary theatre director.

'What's that book for?' she said. 'I always thought you were a fucking amateur.'

I ditched it the next time we did a show. Today I still use the lectern and a few notes, but it's just a crutch. I try to do as much as possible on the hoof and I've found that I prefer it. We play all over the country, and while we try to keep the show topical and relevant to wherever we are,[2] the format is

---

2 For example, if I'm playing a gig in Norwich I always say, 'It's lovely to be back in Norwich. The "w" is silent – as in Paul Anka.' I've done that in Dulwich, Harwich . . . everywhere!

pretty much as it was that first night in Taunton. There seems to be some sort of telepathy between me and Colin, which makes for some wonderful impromptu moments. Now, no show is ever the same twice. There's a lot of material in my head that I've accumulated over the years and often it just comes out at random.[3] It's strange, but it seems that telling jokes and funny stories is so 'out' that it's 'in'. Some younger comedians probably think me of me as 'old school', but I find that if you don't mess with the formula too much you're pretty much guaranteed to give a good couple of hours' worth of entertainment. Some nights, I might get onstage, sniff the air and decide to try out a few topical jokes to see what kind of audience we have. However, I've been booked for an after-dinner speech and occasionally made the mistake of doing a joke from a news report I've just watched while waiting to go on. The audience is confused because they were in the bar while the TV was on. I always say that you should do a topical joke tomorrow.

I try to keep my material varied in the shows with Colin, but there are some lines I won't cross. I did a few Amy Winehouse jokes for a while but I stopped when she started to become something of a lost soul. I've never been a racist or sexist comedian, but I was once accused of sexism after a show for telling a joke about a woman driver. I went away, thought about it, and it struck me that it didn't matter what the sex was, it was just a joke about a stupid driver. So I changed it to a man and it went down just as well when I next told it.

---

3 Still sound familiar?

After a few years, we decided to freshen up the show on the advice of David Foster, who does all our bookings for us. We changed a few things, dropped some older material from the running order and kept a few of the classic stories and gags to bring out towards the end. I like these, as they're a kind of comfortable cushion, a collection of 'greatest hits' that buffer up well against newer material.

Barry Cryer's Greatest Hits: Volume One

Number 59: The Moths Joke

A woman is in bed with a man she shouldn't be in bed with and all is well with the world until her husband comes home unexpectedly. Her lover flees into the bathroom and hides behind the shower curtain. The woman's husband enters the bedroom and kisses his wife.

Wife: Come to bed, darling.
Husband: I will. I'll just pop in the bathroom.
No amount of pleading from her can change his mind, so he goes into the bathroom and pulls back the curtain to reveal a man, barefoot to the neck, tapping the wall and clapping.
Husband: Who are you?
Lover: Council. (*Beat*) Your wife rang up and said that the flat was infested with moths.
Husband: But, you're naked.
The lover looks down.
Lover: The bastards!

One night, I started to tell the joke and a man at the front shouted, 'I love this one!' So I invited him up to tell it with me. I started the joke, then pointed at him for the next line and on it went. I gave him the punchline and he was delighted.

One thing I did do for the newly revised show, which I instantly regretted, was to get rid of 'The Bucket'. This is simply a plastic bucket placed in the foyer before a show with pens and slips of paper next to it. The audience is invited to write a word, a phrase or a question, and in the second half of the show I draw out the slips of paper and see if I can associate a gag or a story with whatever's on the paper. In the interests of variety I dropped this when we changed the show and swapped it for a section where people shouted out the page number of a book, and I'd find a word that I could improvise with. I used to vary this by getting them to shout out a letter once I'd arrived on the page, so it would be narrowed down, but weirdly they always seemed to shout out the same letters – A, B, N and M. Eventually, I decided to reintroduce the good old bucket. It's more fun, it gets the audience involved and it keeps me on my toes. It's my favourite part of the show because it's the part which belongs to the audience. You do get the weirdest things written sometimes, but they bring out the stories. I do get thrown by it, though. One night I pulled out a slip which said 'shirts'. I looked at Colin, he looked at me and we both knew I was about to dry up. Then I said, 'There was this farmer – who was wearing a shirt – and one day . . .' The audience forgives you if you can bend it around, even if it's completely unsubtle. It's part of the fun. The audience being of a certain age, shall we say, I get a lot of questions about 'Clue', Humph, Morecambe and Wise, Tommy Cooper and the rest.

This show is nothing less than a joy for me. I started as a stand-up, then became a writer and now I'm a performer again, so it's gone full circle. I'm very lucky, because there are many talented people my age – and considerably younger – who can't get arrested for what they do, and they're having a hell of a time. I just hope I'm good value, and that I continue to be soon for as long as I can.

The Oldie

I once spoke at a lunch where the guest of honour was Gene Kelly. I looked at him and said, 'I'm working on a new British stage musical – an underwater version of *The Hunchback of Notre Dame*. It's entitled "Ringing in the Seine".' Say it out loud. They didn't laugh much then, either.

Once a month, or thereabouts, I have the great pleasure of being invited to *The Oldie* magazine's literary lunch, held at Simpson's-in-the-Strand restaurant in London. I've also spoken at a couple of them. More often than not, though, I simply go along for the good food and great conversation. However, sometimes, there's no such thing as a free lunch.

I wrote a book some years ago and was invited by *Oldie* editor Richard Ingrams to speak about it at a lunch. I did, and was duly invited back as a non-speaking guest a few months later. As I arrived, Ben Tisdall, who was the events organiser for the magazine, greeted me at the door.

'Come upstairs for a drink,' he said rather ominously. I was immediately suspicious because drinks in this restaurant are always taken downstairs. I had an odd premonition that the guest of honour might not be turning up. 'Is Spike not coming?' I asked Ben. He nodded. What had this got to do with me? As I entered the bar upstairs, Richard Ingrams came over. 'Baz,' he said, 'I'm afraid that you're Spike Milligan today. Is that all right?' I borrowed pen and paper from the barman and frantically scribbled down as many Spike Milligan stories as I could remember. Anyway, the talk went off reasonably well, in spite of the audience's obvious disappointment at not seeing Spike. After the lunch, Richard came up and thanked me for stepping in at the last minute.

'You're invited to every *Oldie* lunch as a guest,' he said, 'on condition that we can ring you the night before or on the morning and say someone hasn't turned up.'

Well, that was fine with me and I'm very happy to be on their sub's bench arrangement. It's enabled me to meet a wide variety of fascinating people, not just from entertainment but politicians, sportsmen and women, writers, and campaigners.

I met the Calendar Girls at an *Oldie* lunch, quite a few years before their film fame, and some of them subsequently came to see me in Grassington in Yorkshire when I did my one-man show. This was at the time of the foot and mouth outbreak, with the accompanying grim stories of suicides and bankruptcies. It was a horrible time, and we arrived to palls of smoke across the valley and men wandering around in flak jackets. But even in the midst of all of it, a woman said to me, 'We've just been to see that new film *Sheepless in Settle*.'

Lord's Taverners

I've been a Lord's Taverner for a long time. I can't say I'm obsessed with cricket but I was happy to turn out for the

Taverners' charity games.[1] Sometimes the team included the likes of Denis Compton, Bill Edrich, Freddy Trueman and Brian Close; so you were padding up with some idols of the game. Brian Close[2] took the fixtures very seriously and wasn't keen on the fooling around that went on. Colin Cowdrey was once batting and hit an unusually ungainly scooping shot back towards the slow bowler. Fred Trueman was at the non-striker's end and as the ball came towards him, he intercepted it, knocking it for four. The crowd laughed but Brian didn't like it at all. I was once fielding very close to the boundary and I bent down to stop a ball that was zipping towards me. As I did, the flannels that I'd borrowed off my son Tony, split. Cue a big laugh from the crowd, who thought I'd staged it deliberately. I don't think Brian was very impressed then either. As a slow bowler, I was so wayward that batsmen often accused me of ignoring them. As a batsman, I went in at number nine and my walk to the wicket was known as the after-eight mince. As far as I was concerned I was there to do a show. Willie Rushton also played but he took it very seriously because he was a good player. I also turned out for the Taverners with the likes of Richard Stilgoe, Robert Powell and Jasper Carrott. It was always an interesting mix of actors, comics, and great cricketers at the Taverners and I've enjoyed my time with them enormously.

---

1 Even though I was abysmal as a player.
2 Brian once positioned me fielding, and he kept ordering me to go further back. I did, but he called me back, shouting, 'Hold, hold on, I don't go that far for my holidays!'

First Among Prequels

I went to a charity do at a hotel near Hyde Park Corner one afternoon and among the guest speakers was Jeffrey Archer. He stood up and delivered what I thought was five word-perfect minutes of my act. Naturally, I was surprised, but I decided not to pursue the matter. Jeffrey's world is a curious one and I didn't want to enter it over a few gags. The afternoon had brought pleasant weather, so I decided to have a short stroll in the sunshine. I was wandering down Park Lane when I heard footsteps behind me, accompanied by the sound of a famous novelist calling my name.

'Yes, Jeffrey?' I said, as he caught up.

'What did you think?'

Three weeks later, I was invited to one of the famous Friday lunches organised by the late lamented *Punch* magazine. Although I didn't contribute very often, I still managed to make the lunch now and then. A few minutes after I got there, Alan Coren, who was editor then, came over with none other than Jeffrey Archer in tow.

'Jeffrey,' he said, 'have you met Barry Cryer?'

'No,' he replied with a matter-of-fact ease.

Now, maybe he'd genuinely forgotten our conversation three weeks previously or maybe he'd blanked out the experience because of embarrassment. Either way, it's extremely difficult to judge, but I was dumbfounded.

A flamboyant *Oldie* lunch guest was Felix Dennis, the multi-millionaire publisher, who'd become famous during the *Oz* obscenity trial of the 1960s. Felix had just given a speech and it was now the turn of Andrew Roberts, the historian. Andrew started speaking about the First World War and the colonial input from the Australians, New Zealanders and Canadians, when he was interrupted by one of the regulars.

'My father died there,' he shouted, 'and he wasn't too thrilled to be there!'

Before any of us could ascertain what he was going on about, Felix shouted back,

'Yes, and the fucking Maoris weren't too thrilled to be killed either!'

Immediately, a woman stood up and shouted,

'Shut up, we've heard you speak!'

Suddenly it was all going off. Right on cue, Leslie Phillips stood up and said,

'I was going to give a little talk but instead, any questions?'

A more peaceful lunch took place earlier this year, when Andrew Sachs was guest of honour. He'd just been through the mill after the comments made about his granddaughter by Russell Brand and Jonathan Ross. He was given the 'Granddad of the Year Award' and he spoke with the good grace and charm that he's always been associated with.

'I don't often speak in public,' he said, rather self-deprecatingly. 'In fact, I hardly speak at all. The older I get, the less I speak and the more they tell me I'm dignified!'

He was very funny, and he reduced the room to tears of laughter when, at the end, he accepted his award with mock

(top) The Simon Cowell Fan Club

(below) Louis Armstrong (in concert)

Beverley Sisters (early years)

Summer season (Lytham St Annes)

Fishermen

My first laptop

On tour with the Guandong band

Marina Theatre, Lowestoft (early years)

THE SMALLEST THEATRE IN THE WORLD

Away day with the Darby & Joan Club

'Bruce' from Jaws

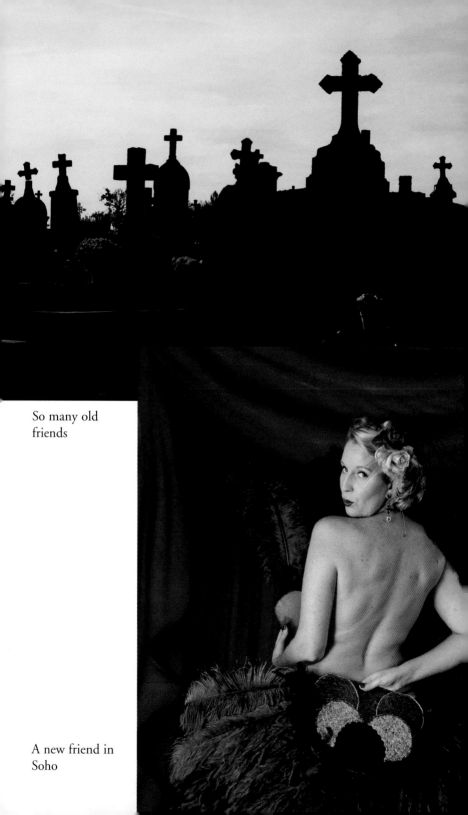

So many old
friends

A new friend in
Soho

Cannon & Balls

To whom I owe
everything

A skeleton.
Springwatch 2007.

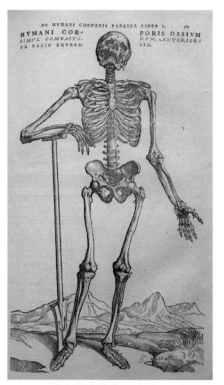

An old man with a
white beard.

tears in his eyes. He wondered where he should start with his list of thank-yous, before thanking 'those wonderful guys' Brand and Ross. He sat down to thunderous applause.

After Dinner Mince

I'm also on the after-dinner speech circuit, and have been since the late 1960s. The first one I did was when I was working for ATV, when the company hosted a dinner at the Café Royal in London. I was told that Lew Grade, the formidable boss of ATV, would be there. I felt somewhat daunted by the prospect of telling gags in front of the great man, but luckily someone tipped me off that while he didn't mind jokes about fat people and rich people, he drew the line at Jewish jokes. 'So, I can do his girth and his worth but not his birth?' I thought. Anyway, the lunch went well and afterwards I sat next to Lew Grade, who was courteous and charming. At one point he said, 'I wonder what I should do with you?' and I suddenly had visions of spectacular offers but sadly, I never heard anything.[1] However, the speech must've fallen on receptive ears somewhere, because soon after I was asked to speak at a Lord's Taverners lunch. The aforementioned Denis Compton and Bill Edrich were there, and it was the first time I ever wrote a poem especially for an occasion, which I've done many times since. I asked the Taverners for some background information on Compton and Edrich and constructed the poem around what they gave

---

1 I have to file it in 'What Might Have Been', along with Boris Karloff, Harold Lloyd and Stanley Kubrick. But that's for another book. And I probably have put those in another book. I just can't remember which one.

me. When I finished, Bill and Denis grabbed my hands and we all stood up with our hands raised in the air.[2]

I started to get more and more requests for after dinners and soon I realised I'd added another string to my bow. Over the years, I've done hundreds of them, for many different companies and organisations and I love the challenge that this variety brings. One such job was at a big event in Harrogate, which had previously attracted star speakers like Bill Clinton and Nelson Mandela. The event was due to be attended by George Bush Snr, and organisers rang me to say that I'd be on 'at quarter to ten'. I said that I thought that was quite late for an after dinner, but he said that he meant '9.45 *a.m.*', explaining that comedy tended to lighten up the guests after *breakfast*. I went up to Harrogate in a state of confusion and stood up at the appointed hour in front of a marquee of well-breakfasted delegates. The organiser was right; it went down very well and I then took part in a live link-up to Hull where I talked to Jacqueline Gold, the woman who runs Ann Summers. A bizarre gig, but very enjoyable. Then the organiser said, 'Bush is here at 3 p.m. and any moment now the place will be crawling with cops and dogs.' I took the hint and left the ex-President in the capable hands of the people of Harrogate.

On another occasion, I've spoken on a topping-out cere-mony on a building in the City of London, complete with hard hat. I read a poem that day too, and it nearly blew away in the wind. I've done one in a small room in a restaurant in front of an audience containing a heavily built guy who was

---

2 I don't always get that reaction.

progressively getting drunk. He kept heckling me, albeit in a friendly way, and when it was obvious I was taking no notice, he got up from his seat, crossed the room, picked me up and plonked me on a woman's lap. I just carried on talking.[3]

I did an after dinner in a hotel outside Lisburn, Northern Ireland, with a friend called Terri Rogers. Terri was a trans-sexual ventriloquist,[4] brilliantly funny and sadly no longer with us. Her doll was very obscene and hilarious, and the whole act was petty extraordinary. Now, this was in the bad old days of the conflict in Northern Ireland and a formidable fence ringed the hotel. The security was just as fearsome, and we seemed to be searched everywhere we went. I was the after-dinner speaker and Terri was the cabaret. Just a few minutes into her act, the hotel manager came on to the stage and told everyone that there was a bomb scare, and the hotel had to be evacuated. We all trooped out of the dining room, through the front door of the hotel and into a kind of hunting lodge in the grounds. For about an hour we amused ourselves by swapping stories and jokes until the manager came back to tell us that the all-clear had been given. He then told Terri that she didn't need to continue her act if she didn't want to. However, being the trouper that she was, Terri insisted on going back on and finishing it. The audience was very pleased, especially when the doll suddenly sat upright on her lap, looked round wide-eyed and said, 'What the fuck was that?'

---

3 If you are the woman in question, I hope your knees are better.
4 A competitive field.

I think this last story shows that you have to be flexible, because people haven't necessarily come to see you. When I'm doing my one-man show, I will put in two hours on-stage, but an after-dinner speech is often no more than about forty minutes long. However, I'm not fooled into thinking that it's any easier. This is partly because you need to be motoring within a few minutes, otherwise you'll quickly lose the audience's attention. It's also because the younger ones often have no idea who I am. I was once told, as I sat at the top table at one dinner with the chairman, that a young sales rep said, 'Who's the white-haired old fart?' When Willie Rushton spoke at after dinners, he used to wait to be called down from his hotel room at the right time. I make a point of going to the meal itself. This is partly because I wouldn't like to just appear from nowhere, only for people to say, 'Oh, here's Barry Took.' I like to mingle, get to know people and pick up snippets of information. You can get your table on your side and find out who the characters are in the room, so that you can refer to them during your speech. People like and appreciate when you've done your homework and put a bit of effort in.

Before I leave the top table, I want to share with you a story about an after dinner I did years ago. Two women asked me afterwards if I wanted a lift home, as I live in Hatch End and they lived in nearby Ruislip. It turned out one of their husbands was in the Round Table. There was going to be a parade that afternoon for charity and the husband had been deputed to tow a paper dragon down the street. The other woman said,

'How did he get stuck with that job?'

She replied, very solemnly and seriously,
'He's the only Round Tabler with a tow bar.'

I told Alan Bennett this and he groaned with laughter. I was rehearsing a show in North Acton three months later, when the lift door opened and Alan stepped out. He looked at me and said,
'He's the only Round Tabler with a tow bar.'

Rock 'n' Droll

Finland, as everyone knows, is the epitome of zeitgeist and good taste when it comes to rock 'n' roll. London? LA? New York? Old hat, I'm afraid. Helsinki's where it's at – or at least it was in 1958, when I released a record over there and it was number one for three weeks. Yes, count them – three whole weeks. Eat your heart out, Bryan Adams. The song was my version of 'The Purple People Eater', a song written by the actor and singer Sheb Woolley which, for contractual reasons, couldn't be released in Finland. Unfortunately, my label, Fontana Records, never took up the option of a second stab at the charts. Instead, my career meandered its merry way elsewhere. But that little taste of rock 'n' roll stardom never quite left me, and today I'm living the dream, rocking it out at Glastonbury, the Edinburgh Festival[1] and anywhere else that's happy to host a show by a bona fide, hit-making, seventy-four-year-old rock star and his sixty-one-year-old mate.

In my teens, like most growing up at that time, I was blown away by the arrival of rock 'n' roll. It made the pop

---

1 Eric Douglas, the son of Kirk, and the brother of Michael, once tried his luck as a stand-up comedian. He did the Edinburgh Festival and his first night was just awful. People were heckling and there was slow hand-clapping. Eric snapped and said, 'Don't you know who I am? I'm Kirk Douglas's son.' And a man in the audience put his hand up and said, 'No, I'm Kirk Douglas's son.' Then the whole audience stood up and shouted the same thing.

played on the radio seem so bland. However, unlike others, my heroes weren't Elvis Presley or Bill Hailey, they were people like Jerry Lee Lewis, Little Richard and Jerry Reed.[2] I also loved the great gospel singers and their accompanying choirs. Even today, a recording of Mahalia Jackson in full flow makes the hairs stand up on the back of my neck. That kind of voice is one that white people can only imitate. I think Tom Jones has a sensational voice that is distinctly Welsh but with strong black influences too, especially in the way he phrases, and uses rhythm. All the great blues and gospel singers know how to use their voices this way.

I don't have much time for cool jazz.[3] I admire it as a style, but I couldn't sit through a whole evening of it. Cool jazz gives people pleasure, obviously, but I like to see showmanship in front of an audience. I think this is what first attracted me to singing when I was at Leeds University. We were writing shows and needed to share out the tasks. I've never had any formal music training and I can't read the dots, but I soon found out that I could learn and sing songs while the more musically gifted accompanied me at the piano. However, I regret not having lessons sometimes as, to this day, Terry tells me that she can sometimes hear that I'm straining my voice. I'd need it if I were to realise an ambition to record something like 'Just a Closer Walk with Thee' with a proper gospel choir. I came close once, on a short-lived show called *Cabaret X*. For it, the producers asked me to reprise the gospel song I did in the *Two Old Farts* show about worshipping

---

2 Who went on to write and record 'Guitar Man'.
3 And it's never had much time for me, apparently.

'Cheeses'.[4] They provided a full backing band, complete with gospel singers, and it was wonderful to hear that particular arrangement of it. I was in heaven.[5]

Some years ago, I decided to ask a friend of mine, Ronnie Golden, whether he fancied teaming up to create a live music show. Now, you might ask, 'Who is Ronnie Golden?'[6] He is a brilliantly underrated[7] performer, songwriter and musician, who has been on the music scene for years. In the late 1970s, he was in a band called The Fabulous Poodles[8] that had a tilt at fame in America.[9] Then he went into comedy and blended that with his music, as well as some theatre and TV work and a band of his own. In short, he's a jack-of-all-trades like me.

I first met him at the Hackney Empire, when he was introduced to me as Ronnie Golden. He told me his real name was Tony De Meur[10] but he'd been Ronnie for so long that it had stuck and there didn't seem to be much point in changing it at that stage.

We kept in touch and I went to see him at the King's Head in Crouch End. I told a few jokes, he did some music and by the end of the show I acknowledged what had been staring me in the face for a while. Ronnie was the perfect partner for a new show. He writes such marvellous comedy songs, and he can play the guitar, ukulele, mandolin, and har-

---

4 I'll wait.
5 Not the nightclub.
6 Most people ask, '*Where* is Ronnie Golden?' but that's a different story.
7 Not by me, I hasten to add.
8 Look up Mirror Stars and Think Pink for unbridled joy.
9 Supporting the Ramones and Tom Petty, no less.
10 An old Huguenot name, which I thought was rather fabulous and a better stage name than Ronnie Golden.

monica. I asked him if he was up for it and to my relief he agreed.

As with Colin, Ronnie came round to my house and we worked on ideas for material. We're both keen on writing lyrics, and whatever I throw at him, he can shape to fit the music. He knows where a middle eight should drop in and where a key change should be. He's also great on melody, and how to pastiche a style effectively.

Once we had enough numbers for about an hour's show it was time to find a venue. We managed to get a late-night slot at the Traverse Theatre in Edinburgh for a week. We really enjoyed the experience but the theatre itself was more geared to plays and, despite the best efforts of the crew, they weren't used to hooligans turning up with guitars and amplifiers. We were keen to do Edinburgh again the following year, and luckily, Karen Coren, who ran the Gilded Balloon, asked us if we wanted a slot. The venue does comedy, music and theatre; exactly what we were looking for.

We put the show together and hoped people would come, and they did. This was a much more diverse audience than the one I'd been getting for the shows with Colin. They were old, young, students, tourists and basically anyone who was up for a laugh and a few songs. It's an all-song show, so I was leaning on Ronnie to an extent to drive it forwards. However, all the time I was thinking what fun it was.

Even though I'd been to the Festival with Willie Rushton, Edinburgh was a revelation to me. I wanted to see as much as I could, but of course, there are thousands of shows and even if you have a great night at one show, you invariably meet someone the following day who tells you that he's seen the greatest performance of his life the previous night, and you've missed it.[11]

These days we go up there for a week. I've done a fortnight in the past, but that can be somewhat gruelling and by the middle of the second week you're longing for a lie-down. What I like doing now is playing the middle week of the Fringe when it's buzzing and everything is still happening. I've seen some tremendous shows in recent years; comedians like Jeremy Hardy and Mike McIntyre, terrific plays, gospel choirs, one-man shows, one-woman shows. The diversity on offer is breathtaking. This year I was asked to do Sheridan's *School for Scandal* but it's a four-week run and I was worried about keeping up the commitment to the show that Ronnie and I do, so I turned it down. Ronnie does three or four things while he's up there, but one show is enough for me.

To date, we've played Edinburgh seven times and in a way, I'm quite proud to be something of a pioneer for the older generation up there. In fact, quite a few entertainers of a certain age have asked me, on the quiet, what it is like to play the Fringe. I've told them that it's fun, and that if you've still got the energy and the wherewithal to make a show and perform it, it's the perfect place. It's a reality now that TV won't give older performers the opportunities they used to.

---

11 That's not to say that they're all hits. A few years ago at Edinburgh, a comedian was doing a routine in which he played all the *Star Trek* characters. It wasn't going well, and a voice in the audience said, 'This is comedy, Jim, but not as we know it.'

That's understandable, as fashions change, but I wish that when they do make programmes about older people, they're not quite so patronising. My generation doesn't feel old and while we don't expect the lion's share of the schedules, we'd like to be represented as still having something to offer. So maybe TV's loss is Edinburgh's gain. Hopefully, live theatres can provide the platform for more voices of my generation. Judging by who I've spoken to, there's certainly a long list to choose from.

I met John Stannah, the boss of Stannah Stairlifts, at an *Oldie* lunch and he asked me what I was up to. I told him about my show with Ronnie, we chatted about it, and I thought no more of it, until I got a call a few days after. John was offering to sponsor the show. I had little hesitation in agreeing, thinking it would provide rich comedy material. On the opening night I made reference to the fact that we were the only show on the Fringe to be sponsored by Stannah. A lot of people thought we were joking and we even did a song about it. We still do it, and Stannah loves it.

In fact, Ronnie and I tend to write about whatever takes our fancy. Topicality is always high up the agenda, and there's enough going on in any given summer to fill a few hours. We did a song in Edinburgh called 'Bono', which was a paean to a great prophet who descends to earth from on high.[12]

---

12 I bet you've no idea who we could be talking about.

Bono

We were down and we were troubled
We had no purpose, we saw no goal
We'd lost our way, where were we going?
Where was our heart? Where was our soul?
But one day we got the message
We were transformed, so praise the Lord!
At last we'd found the answer
We would march on to our reward
In these times of tribulation
We need someone to show the way
Who can lead us to redemption
On that great and glorious day
We saw the light, the heavens opened
And then He came into view
He cried out, 'God bless you, children!'
We replied, 'God bless U2!'
We'd found Bono, and we were thankful that he came
It took a while to find him, the streets all had no name
God bless you, Bono, sing hallelujah and sing in praise
And just like God, you move in mysterious ways
God bless you, Bono, God bless Geldof and The Edge
Though we're not worthy we give you blessing
And we make this solemn pledge:
We will follow where you lead us
Sing hallelujah, sing in praise
Just like God you move in mysterious ways.

Because we're in Scotland, we do a song called 'Scot Free',

which is a mock salute to the pride of Little Englanders and the Scottish influence in their politics and media.

Scot Free

This precious jewel set in a silver sea, this green and pleasant
Land of the free; united by the bonds we forge
Beneath our flag, God bless St George
So today we bend the knee before our rulers
Therefore we will name them proudly, take our stand
All hail the masters of our land
Leader Blair from Morningside
He wears his Fettes badge with pride
The Chancellor, good Gordon Brown, the fine son of
    Kirkcaldy town
John Reid of Glasgow straight and true
Lord Falconer, Lord Chancellor, who
Joins Lord Irving, son of Inverness,
Alistair Darling, how we bless
These names, Des Browne, secretary of state, from Ayrshire,
Proud to relate; Ian McCartney, Party chair, Michael Martin,
    the Speaker there
Among 106 MPs, all Scots are they and keen to see
The power that they proudly wield
From far and wide, a fruitful field
The medium, James Naughtie in the morn
Andrew Marr, Glasgow, born
Andrew Neil and Nicky Campbell, the list is endless
As I ramble on

Hail Kirsties Wark and Young
From Dumfries and Lanark have they sprung
Kirsty Wark from low to high land, Kirsty Young on her
   Desert Island
There will always be an England, proud and free
But never, ever quite Scot free.[13]

We've also done the Glastonbury Festival, and although I'm still finding mud in my socks, it was a wonderful, once-in-a-lifetime experience. What they say about those fields in Somerset is true; you don't walk on mud, you walk through it. We were playing in the comedy tent and after we parked the car, we slithered down a hill to where we were headed. Ronnie was in his element because this was Glastonbury. I thought it was quite a spectacle, but I was a little less sure of the cardboard dressing room and the duckboards across the mud that led to the stage. Luckily I spotted a BBC caravan nearby so I went over and sweet-talked them into letting us change in it.

We had T-shirts on that said 'Old's Cool'[14] and just before we walked across the duckboards to take the stage, our weight caused the mud to spurt up and spatter us. At least we looked like Glastonbury veterans by the time we arrived. I was pleased that we'd been there and made a success of it, and I was particularly pleased for Ronnie because I knew it meant a lot to him. Ronnie decided to stay for the weekend, but I was working the following day and I didn't really relish

---

13 At this point imagine bagpipes creeping in. If you dare. But keep the noise down because of the neighbours.
14 Geddit? No? Ask Lynne Truss.

the thought of being jammed face downwards in a cow field for a weekend.[15] The organisers arranged for a Land Rover to take me back to the car. Now, as many Glastonbury survivors will attest, parking a car in a huge field full of other cars in daylight is one thing, but locating it again at night is quite another. Eventually the car was found and although it took an hour to get off the site it was worth the wait. I slept in a warm, dry bed that night while Ronnie and his rock 'n' roll mates stayed in a tent that slid in the mud as they slept.

Live performing is wonderful and it suits me down to the ground. As I've said, I couldn't be an actor, turning up to the same venue every night to say the same lines, for weeks or months on end. I'm more of a hit and run man; do the show, move on, next town.[16]

---

15 Although I don't think that's obligatory.
16 A bit like a cat burglar. Just with less fur balls.

Second Interval[1]

This will be followed by a selection of footnotes that didn't make it into the book. For fun, just imagine the many hilarious passages of my life that the following stories could apply to:[2]

1.   Sir Robert Fellowes, brother-in-law of the late Princess Diana, was personal private secretary to the Queen. This is a true apocryphal story. He was making his way through customs at Sydney airport and handed over his passport. In those days you had to fill in your occupation so with a certain grandeur he'd put 'courtier'. And the man looked at it, handed it back and said, 'There's no "t" in courier, mate.'

2.   A man walking across the terminal at Sydney airport slid in some dog-doo on the floor. A security man came up and said, 'Sorry about that, mate, one of our dogs thought he'd found a bomb.'

3.   Roy Castle told me about the Record Breakers show where they attempted to stage the biggest musical chairs in the world.

---

1 A bit like the first, but this time taken from the RSC's recent production of *Titus Andronicus*. Slightly less laughs than *King Lear* but with tastier pies.
2 Whilst remembering that they are, in no way, a loose affiliation of jokes and stories that I couldn't crowbar elsewhere into the book. Any suggestion in this direction will be met with a strongly worded letter.

There were scores of competitors, bands, and a huge crowd. Finally came the dramatic finale, and he said that he never forgot, after all the elimination and the music stopping and starting, watching one man circling two chairs.

4.   A comedian called Johnny Hammond was in a boxing ring one night, telling jokes. A boxer called Terry Downes got into the ring, grabbed the mic from him and said, 'You've been in this ring too long.' And Johnny said, 'Longer than you ever were.'

5.   Miles Jupp, theological student turned stand-up, told me he was doing his act in the back of a pub and he was being heckled. He made his way out of the pub after the show and the big bouncer said, 'Miles, the guy who heckled you is outside, I've switched the CCTV off if you want to take a pop at him.' If you've ever met Miles Jupp, you couldn't imagine anyone less likely to 'take a pop' at anyone.

6.   I have a friend, a journalist called Revel Barker who is well over 6ft 5. He was with a woman one night who said, 'Revel, are you all in proportion?' And he said, 'No, love. If I was I'd be 9ft 10.'

7.   Speaking of which, a little boy was walking round a zoo with his mum. They walked past the elephant enclosure, and there was a male elephant in a state of high arousal. 'What's that?' the little boy said to his mother. 'Oh, nothing,' said the mother, and they walked on. Later on, the little boy was with his father. They saw the same elephant and the boy said, 'Mummy said that was nothing.' And his father said, 'Well, your mother's been spoilt.'

8.   A journalist went to interview a well-known politician. His wife came to the door and she said, 'He's upstairs, he'll be down in a minute.' The journalist looked round and noticed a portrait of Ken Dodd on the wall. The politician came down the stairs and the journalist says, 'What's that picture of Doddy doing there?' 'That's my wife,' the politician replied.

9.   A teacher asked some boys what their dads did for a living. 'Builder', 'Doctor', 'Lawyer', they replied. One said, 'My dad's a pole dancer in a bondage club.' 'Is that true?' the teacher said to the boy. 'No,' the boy replied, 'he's a banker, but I'm too embarrassed to say it.'

10.   Picasso was once burgled, he arrived back at his house and the burglar was still there but made his escape through a window. Picasso saw him as he ran off and did a drawing of him to help the police. The next day they arrested a horse and two sardines.

11.   Quentin Crisp eventually went to live in America, and somebody asked him why. He said, 'Americans say "have a nice day" and they don't mean it. The English say, "piss off" and they do.'

12.   Ronald Reagan used to tell the story of the two men in the woods, who were chased by a bear. One man started to flee, but the other man bent down to lace up his shoes. And the first man said, 'You'll never outrun a bear!' and the other man said, 'I just have to outrun you.'

13.   Walter Matthau and Jack Lemmon were making a film and

Walter collapsed with a heart attack. The doctor was summoned and Jack was cradling his old friend. 'Are you comfortable, Walter?' he said. Walter replied, 'I make a living.'

14.   Janet Suzman, the actress, told me of the time she was touring in *Hedda Gabler*. When the dramatic moment came for Hedda to storm off, they used a tape of a piano playing offstage. They arrived at the Grand Theatre in Leeds, and someone had forgotten the tape. The theatre reassured them that they could use one of theirs. On the first night, Janet stormed off the stage and to hear a click and a voice, saying, 'The curtain will rise in three minutes.'

15.   Groucho Marx's daughter wanted to join a club, and this club would never have admitted to being anti-semitic, it was just that they had no Jewish members. And Groucho was furious. He wrote to the club and said, 'For your information my daughter is half-Jewish. Can she go in your pool up to her waist?'

16.   A very diffident little man went to a party without his wife and during the party they had to draw bits of paper out of a hat and make a speech about the word written on the paper. He drew 'sex' and spoke for several minutes. Everyone laughed and it was a fun evening. Then he went home and his wife asked how the party was. 'We played a game where we had to draw paper out of a hat and speak on a subject,' he said. 'What did you choose?' she asked. He panicked and said the first thing that came into his head – 'Yachting.' The next day the wife was out shopping and she met a woman who had been at the party. 'Your husband was very funny last night,' said the woman. 'I don't understand it,'

replied the wife, 'he's only done it three times. First time he was sick. The second time his hat blew off. The third time he was winched off by helicopter.'

Funerals, Memorials and Other Happy Tales

According to most studies, people's number one fear is public speaking. Number two is death. Death is number two. Does that sound right? This means to the average person, if you go to a funeral, you're better off in the casket than doing the eulogy.

JERRY SEINFELD

I've lost some good friends over the years and each one has been a very personal and deep loss. Whilst the death of an old friend is obviously very sad, and although I don't want to appear to be making light of this fact, the fact remains that many of these friends would have treated their own deaths with as much irreverence as they would have treated their lives. As a result, memorial services have now become places where being maudlin seems out of fashion.

If, like me, you're asked to speak at these occasions, then you tread a narrow tightrope. You have to remember that family are present, and while you want to stay as true to the spirit of the deceased as possible, there might be certain things you really can't say. That said, and to quote John Cleese at the memorial service for Graham Chapman in 1989, you'd rather say 'anything but mindless good taste'.

Graham's memorial has become a benchmark by which all other services are now judged. It hit the headlines, not simply because it was Graham but because John Cleese allegedly became the first person to say 'fuck' at a British memorial service. I was asked by Graham to be MC at that service and when John so deliberately and carefully enunciated that word, from the front of the Great Hall at St Bartholomew's Hospital, the shock, mixed with laughter from the congregation, was incredible. It was spot on because Graham wouldn't have wanted it any other way.

Alfred Drayton

Years ago, before the Second World War, there was a series of shows in London called the Aldwych Farces, named after the theatre they were performed in. A stalwart of the cast was an actor called Alfred Drayton, who was a formidable-looking man with a shaved head. As a kind of Telly Savalas of his day, he always played villains and heavies and was a favourite among audiences. Then, rather unfortunately, he died during rehearsals for one of the shows. The company found itself bereft of a popular character and at the last minute they drafted in an actor called Arthur Riscoe.

Arthur was a bit of a tippler but he was so pleased to get the part that he stayed on the wagon and learned his lines thoroughly. The day of Alfred Drayton's funeral came and, out of courtesy, the rest of the cast asked Arthur along to the service at Golders Green crematorium. He was somewhat nervous, having to attend the funeral of the actor he was replacing, but he got through it. Afterwards, they all decided to have a drink at the nearby Bull and Bush pub, Arthur included. As they sat drinking, a fire engine roared past with its bell clanging. It all got a bit too much for Arthur and he suddenly jumped to his feet. 'My God,' he shouted, 'they're putting him out!'

Willie Rushton

Willie Rushton's death in 1996 was very sad for me, because not only had we been friends for so many years, but we'd also only just performed a show together. At the time of his death, I'd just started rehearsing a pantomime in Cambridge, so I came back to London in something of a fluster for his funeral. Apparently one of the last things he said to his wife before he died was, 'Tell Bazza he's too old to do pantomime.' I was asked to speak at the funeral, so I dug out some lyrics that Will had written for our show. I had them printed on eight feet long fax paper which I rolled up very tightly and put in my suit pocket. When it was my turn to speak, I let it unroll all the way to the floor and it got a laugh. After the funeral Tim Brooke-Taylor came up to me. 'How did you manage to get through that?' he asked. It's still a good question. I don't know how I did it as I was feeling terrible inside.

I spoke again at Will's memorial service, held at St Paul's Church, Covent Garden. The day before, news broke that the presenter Hughie Green was the real father of TV personality Paula Yates. Here was the potential for a joke, but I paced up and down before the service, cigarette in hand, wondering whether to do it. I decided that Will wouldn't want any reverence. The church was packed and Ned Sherrin was the MC. He beckoned me up, and I broke the ice by saying, 'I can exclusively reveal today that Willie Rushton was the father of Chris Evans.' Well, I've almost broken out into a sweat remembering that moment, but it got a laugh. As I've said, it's a fine line that you tread but where Will was concerned it could be stepped over, albeit delicately.[1]

Tommy Cooper

I didn't go to Tommy Cooper's funeral as it was a private family affair. However, I remember the horrible feeling of seeing his death live on TV. On the evening of 15 April 1984, I sat down to watch Tom on the show 'Live from Her Majesty's'. I knew that he hadn't been well and that he was drinking a lot, but while his voice was more guttural than usual, he was still getting laughs. The man was a true great, right to the very end. During the performance, he put on a robe and I waited for him to start a few of his terrible tricks. Then he sank to his knees and fell over backwards. I knew something was very wrong because that had never been part of his act. There was an agonising pause, then the band

---

1 I'd like to finish my memories of Will with a rather sweet story of his little-known love of animals. Will was devoted to his cat and he talked with his pet every morning about current affairs and matters of the day. One summer's morning he was sitting there, chatting to the cat, when a moth flew in through the open window, landing on the settee. 'Good morning to you,' Will said to the moth, and chatted away until the moth flew out of the window, obviously bored and in search of another appointment. He turned to the cat and said, 'I'm going mad, I've just been talking to a moth.'

started playing, and they cut to the commercials. When they returned, Jimmy Tarbuck was on, doing his best to paper over the cracks, but it was clear something awful had happened.

Later, I switched on the news and saw that Tom had died. The phone rang.

'Hello, Mr Cryer,' said a voice, 'I'm ringing from ITN.'

'I expect it's about Tommy Cooper,' I replied, getting ready to offer up a few anecdotes about him.

'Yes, it is,' said the voice. 'We were wondering whether you had Eric Morecambe's phone number.'

I lied and said I hadn't got it. Then I rang Eric to tell him, and we spent a few minutes chatting about Tom.

'What a terrible thing to happen to poor Tom,' Eric said. 'And in front of an audience too. I'd never do that. They'll all be saying tomorrow "what a wonderful way to go". There is no wonderful way to go.'

Eric Morecambe

Six weeks later, Eric was doing an 'Audience With' show at a theatre in Tewkesbury. He did a great show and made several curtain calls, coming back on again to comically interrupt the band by larking about with their instruments. He left the stage a final time, had a massive heart attack at the top of the stage steps, and died.

It was hard not to shed a tear when Ernie Wise spoke at Eric's funeral. He looked behind him sadly, saying, 'I keep getting this feeling that he's walking behind me, wearing a raincoat and carrying a shopping bag.' The whole of Harpenden, the town in Hertfordshire where Eric lived, came to a standstill on that day. The church was packed, the streets were full, and the police were diverting the traffic. We were looking at all the floral tributes that had arrived, and among them was even one from the local Chinese takeaway. Eric loved that little town and his feelings were reciprocated in many other tributes like that one.

I'll leave you with one of my favourite moments from 'The Morecambe & Wise Show'. Vera Lynn appeared on the show and we had this idea of writing a script which got her to come on and look stunned when they asked her to sing. She came on to enormous applause and Ernie said, 'What are you going to sing for us, Vera?' She looked rather surprised and said, 'No one's mentioned this.' Ernie looked panicked, so Eric said, 'Can I have a word with you a moment?' So they went to the side of the stage and Ernie said, 'What are we going to do?' and Eric said, 'Short of starting another war, I've no idea.'[2]

Kenny Everett

At Kenny Everett's funeral, I did a reading from the Bible. It was strange, I had the same feelings that Ernie had at Eric's funeral. I half expected the coffin lid to suddenly burst open and Ev to leap out shouting, 'Hello! April Fool!' Before the

---

2 Ken Dodd said he knew the Falklands War was about to start because he walked past Vera Lynn's house and heard her gargling.

service, I was stood outside the church with Ev's agent. A helicopter swooped low over us and in unison we said, 'He's late again.'

Bill Cotton

Earlier this year, I went to St Martin-in-the-Fields in Trafalgar Square to pay my respects to the late Bill Cotton, the former head of light entertainment at the BBC. The church was packed and there were so many well-known faces there it was like 'This Is Your Life'. One of the highlights of his memorial service was a performance by the superb Ukelele Orchestra of Great Britain. They do a huge variety of songs and tunes, all on ukulele, and they seem to be able to play anything, from rock to classical. Bill's dad, Billy Cotton, was a famous dance band leader and he'd famously done an arrangement of the Dambusters March with his band. The Ukelele Orchestra recreated this and it was just astonishing. Then they set off into a dirge that initially sounded very heavy and Russian, until you realised it was George Formby's 'Leaning on a Lamp Post'.[3]

Bill Cotton was a marvellous character who nurtured the talent he employed and got the best out of them largely through encouragement. His solution to every performer's crisis was to take them to his favourite Chinese restaurant.

---

3 Benito Mussolini's recording of 'I'm Hanging from a Lamp Post at the Corner of the Street' inspired George. Formby was Lancashire's answer to Bob Dylan. He could make the ukulele talk, and when it spoke it said, 'For God's sake leave me alone!' And before anyone writes in, I know that he played a banjelele.

At his memorial, someone remarked that Bill preferred crispy duck to psychotherapy.[4]

David Attenborough told a lovely story from Bill's days as head of light entertainment. At the time, there was a BBC boss called Tom Sloan, who, with his blazer and moustache, was rather old school. The Eurovision Song Contest was in its infancy and while the BBC had agreed to televise it, there were a few concerns from those I referred to earlier as the 'blazerati'. Tom, in particular, was quite worried about various aspects of the show, and one day Bill went into Tom's office and told him that Albania would like to be included.

'That's ridiculous!' said Tom. 'They're not even in Euro-vision. They're the wrong side of the Iron Curtain!'

'Well,' said Bill, looking concerned, 'they really want to be in it, so much so that they've staged a demonstration outside.'

Right on cue, three men and a woman, all dressed in East European peasant garb, burst through the office door and began singing a song in a language of no fixed origin. Tom looked more closely, noticing that Bill's staff were the demonstrating musicians. The whole thing was a classic Bill Cotton wind-up. Tom saw the funny side, and the stunt helped to diffuse any tension remaining over the issue.

The last time I met Bill, Terry and I were at a function and he came over to speak to us. He was as warm and effusive as ever. He then said to someone standing nearby,

---

4 If you're reading this and it was you, send me a postcard.

'Have you met this man? He's got it all. He writes, he performs, he sings. There's only one Barry Took.'

My overriding memory of Bill is of him laughing all the time. Although he was never a performer, you could have been fooled into thinking he was. Perhaps he'd inherited the performing gene from his dad or maybe he was simply an extrovert who liked performers and appreciated what they did. Whichever he was, he was a rare breed, because you don't come across many laughing TV executives these days. Bill would remember that a comedian hadn't been on TV for a while, then simply ring him up, arrange lunch, and during the course of it, commission six shows.[5] Bill and his ilk were autocratic and disdainful of TV by committee, but they didn't half get things done. Bill once saw a show in Holland and bought it for the BBC. It was the 'Generation Game'. He decided it would be perfect for Bruce Forsyth. It pulled Brucie out of the doldrums, after his great days at the London Palladium, and made him a TV star.

Paul Schofield

Sadly, only a week after Bill Cotton's memorial, I was at Paul Schofield's. He was such a great actor and as you'd expect, there was a big turnout from the theatrical establishment. It was held in St Margaret's Church, next to Westminster Abbey, but unlike the gathering for Bill, there were hardly

---

5 These days, it would take three months of meetings just to arrange the lunch.

any laughs that day. Personally, I thought that was a shame, because my memories of Paul were ones filled with fun and laughter. I met him in 1958 when he and I were in *Expresso Bongo*. We eventually took the show on tour and Paul's dressing room door was always open. 'Don't say hello, then,' he'd shout as you walked past. He wasn't the least bit grand. The set was very minimalist and there was a scene featuring Millicent Martin set in a flat. Paul was required to come through the door of this flat and casually kick it shut. On the first night, in Newcastle, he did just that and the whole thing fell over, crashing on to the stage and unleashing a huge cloud of dust. Paul surveyed the wreckage. 'Mice,' he said. The cast was somewhat in awe of him because he'd already made a couple of films and had appeared with the Royal Shakespeare Company. However, he was very down to earth and a lovely person to work with.

I made a point of begging, borrowing, buying or stealing a new garish kipper tie for each performance. Paul was an excellent ventriloquist and when I walked on with the new tie, he'd say, 'Where the fuck did you get that – it's awful,' without moving his lips. I found out later that he was also notorious for playing practical jokes on other actors. He once played Lear and, using a fine pen, a mirror and a lot of care, wrote 'Fuck This' on his eyelids. Another story goes that he was once in Moscow playing Hamlet and sat in the front row were a host of earnest students, following the play with books. One night, Paul decided to liven things up and listed the stations of the Northern Line in a speech, smiling as he watched the pages flap in the front row.

Peter Tinniswood

There was a memorial for Peter Tinniswood, an old friend and scriptwriting colleague, following his death in 2003. I was asked by his family to get up and lead the audience in a rendition of 'We'll Meet Again'. At the service was a veteran radio producer called Enid Williams, who told me that at one point a man slid on to the bench next to her. It was Paul Schofield. 'When you got up,' Enid said, 'and you started leading the audience in the song, Paul leaned over and said, "I've worked with him." I'll bet that's made your day!' she said.

Bob Monkhouse

My wife and I were part of the massive turnout for Bob Monkhouse's funeral. There was a songwriter there called Mitch Murray. There was the usual courtesy of letting the family go into the chapel first, but somehow Mitch got caught up in the party by accident. A man came up to him and said, 'Excuse me, are you on the list?' Apparently Mitch said, 'I certainly am, I'm one of the people being cremated this afternoon.'

Larry Stevens

Spike Milligan, Michael Bentine and Peter Sellers went to the funeral of a writer called Larry Stevens, who worked with them on the early days of the Goons. They were sitting in the pew, waiting for it to start, when Spike began to moan, putting his head in his hands. People thought that he was consumed with grief. But Spike wasn't crying, he was laughing. He'd just seen a sign to show where the nearest fire extinguisher was. In a crematorium.

Ode to Spike

I wish I was here with my muse for Milligan
To know and feel the sensual thrill again
To feel once more the song and trill again
The warmth and occasional chill again
To drink a toast and have my fill again
To joyfully take up my quill again
Fortified by a fix or a pill again
Tread my feet on the mill again
Shoot the joke and fire to kill again
To make them laugh as t'were Jack and Jill again
Toast dear Spike upon the grill again
The definitive one-off, the comedy master
The clowning cake, the gateau blaster
The real loose cannon, firing balls
Upon each target, my heart calls
To now salute him, no one like
The one, the inimitable – oh, sod it, Spike!

John Cryer

My brother John died and his funeral was in Tonbridge, Kent. It was a typical funeral day, windy and raining. A lot of old aunties had made the trip down from Leeds. A young local vicar gave the service, and although he hardly knew my brother, he gave a very nice address, which pleased the family. Then he launched into the Lord's Prayer, and as he came to the end you could hear that he had a tickle in his throat. Instead of clearing it, he bravely ended the prayer with 'in the name of the Father, the Son and the Ho-ho-ho-ho-ho . . .' My wife's elbow quickly went into my ribs as my face began to crease.

It had reminded me of a story about a Marty Feldman funeral sketch. They were shooting on location at a church and Marty was dressed in a priest's traditional garb, complete with biretta on his head. He'd just got changed in his caravan and as he came round the corner, he was confronted by a group of people dressed in black. He assumed they were extras for the sketch, so he lifted his skirt and shouted, 'Good morning girls!' The mourners, who had just left the church where a real funeral had taken place, moved on quietly.

Alec Bishop

I also spoke at the funeral of my brother-in-law, Alec Bishop. Now, I loved the man dearly but it's fair to say that, as he was quite a literal chap, our senses of humour were very different. We were gathered round our kitchen table one evening years ago, and I told a joke I'd heard from Frank Carson. It concerned the real case of an Irish Roman Catholic bishop, Eamon Casey, who was discovered to have fathered a child. The joke goes that Casey is in bed with a woman who says, 'I didn't know you were a bishop,' and he says, 'You don't see many plumbers wearing a hat like this.' I told this joke and everyone laughed except my brother-in-law who said, 'Wearing a hat in bed? Surely not.' When he died, his wife Pat insisted that I tell that story. It was Alec to a tee, and those who loved him appreciated it.

Linda Smith

Sometimes at a memorial, it's good to wrong-foot people. Ronnie Golden and I went to Linda Smith's memorial at the Theatre Royal, Stratford East, a month after she died of cancer in 2006. Linda had been a regular panellist on 'Clue' for a few years and we'd all got to know and love her, so the fact that she had so much ahead of her and had died so young was particularly cruel. Ronnie and I were asked to do a song in Linda's memory and because it was one she particularly liked, we did 'Peace and Quiet'. It starts with me talking very quietly about walking through the fury of a storm. Ronnie then begins to strum his guitar, again very quietly. Then I talk about the thunder starting to roll and the song goes louder and louder until it reaches a crescendo and we're screaming at the top of our lungs in the final chorus. The comedian Sean Lock was in the audience that day and afterwards he told me that when we began the song, he couldn't believe he was listening to something so schmaltzy. It took him two verses before he got the joke. I also read out a poem in Linda's memory that day, and here it is:

A Lot of Laughs

Oh, what a happy day to think of Linda
I am so old, I remember Tommy Trinder
You may say: 'Who?', that will not hinder
My verse, because dear Linda
Was in the family line, kith and kinder
That she carried on – Linda Smith
No false memories, no transient myth
She was there, upon the 'News Quiz'
Doing the business, doing the biz
Full of fun and full of fizz
Then thoughts turn to 'Just a Minute'
Who but our own Linda in it
Could fill the seconds with such thoughts
Any context, any sorts
Of reactions were just hers
So many, now my memory blurs
But that's irrelevant, forget the blur
When we remember Linda, it's just her
Funny, natural, endlessly inventive
I don't need any further incentive
To say that you were one of a kind
I can never lose from my mind

Your wit, spontaneously, seemingly unplanned
Your album of whale song that turned out to be
A dolphin tribute band
That's just one and so were you
You always, always had a 'Clue'
And now, my friends, I end this rhyme
Hoping it wasn't a Short History of Wasting Time
With all here, I'm one who has
Lovely memories, love Uncle Baz.

Hatch End

There was no respect for youth when I was young, and now that I am old, there is no respect for age; I missed it coming and going.

J.B. PRIESTLEY

When we were first married, Terry and I lived in a flat in Maida Vale but we were paying nine guineas a week in rent and the family had started to expand. So she decided it was time we went house hunting, and I was sent out to do the business.

We came to Hatch End because of Ronnie Barker.[1] I'd looked at areas south of the river like Roehampton, Putney and Barnes, but nothing had seemed suitable. Ronnie lived in Pinner, and he loved the place and I agreed to go with him one night for a drive around the neighbourhood. I spotted a house for sale and later on, I sat in its living room, drinking a cup of

---

[1] The first ever Comedy Award saw Ronnie Barker given a Lifetime Achievement Award. Sir Alec Guinness was a great fan of Ronnie's, and was asked to present the award. He decided that before introducing Ronnie Barker he'd tell a 'Two Ronnies' joke. The joke in the original is: 'Four men who robbed a bank, fell into a concrete mixer as they made their getaway. They climbed out and ran away. The police are now looking for four hardened criminals.' On stage that night, Alec Guinness said, 'Four men robbed a bank, they made their getaway, crashed into a concrete mixer and fell in. They climbed out and ran away. Police are looking for ... four concrete men.' There's a stunned silence then an enormous laugh. Afterwards, Alec Guinness rang the producer Michael Hurll and said, 'I'll come again and do it right. I'll even wear the same suit.'

tea with the musician owner who was desperate to move. I'd once asked a friend how to go about buying a house and I was told you had to haggle. I managed to beat him down from £11,000 to £10,400. I was a dubious bet for a mortgage but a solicitor friend helped swing it for me. That was in 1967 and we've lived here ever since. I wouldn't move for the world.

The house had been used as lodgings and, therefore, had been divided into sections. When we moved in, it was dark, airless and stripped back to the floorboards. There was a slightly eerie moment when one of the builders, who helped us to open the place up, found a doll dressed as a nun, complete with a broken neck. However, the whole place felt right. Next to the main house, there was an annexe that had been the previous owner's music room. We had it converted into living accommodation for my mother, who lived in it until her death in 1982. Quite a few other houses in our avenue have been converted into flats and although this seems to be an ongoing trend, Terry and I joke that we'll be the old couple in the deckchairs, watching it all happen and resisting all offers from developers.

When we came here, Hatch End had a village atmosphere, and while quite a few of the small shops have gone, to be replaced by a supermarket and a string of restaurants, it still feels very much that way to me. It's probably because so many of the people have become our friends. It doesn't feel anonymous like London, but neither is it countryside. Greenery is there on the doorstep if we want it, but I'd go mad if I lived in the countryside. That was never an option for me as I need to see people. This is the best of both worlds, because I know so many people here and we're a stone's throw away from the station, which means I can be in London in about 35 minutes. It's the perfect combination, and the kind of place I always wanted to live in.

I enjoy my local pub, which used to be Barclays Bank but makes a better pub, and is full of atmosphere and friendly laughter. There used to be one across the road called the Railway, which I used to frequent (although I didn't like it all that much) until it shut down and became a Tesco store. I went in there one night straight from the station and I was standing at the bar, minding my own business, when a voice behind me said,

'Who's the bloke with the beard?'

'Oh, that's the pub bore,' came the reply from elsewhere.

I turned round, assuming it was a regular briefing a visitor and taking the piss. Funny old place, the Railway. There was once a sweepstake there on the Grand National, and to enter you wrote your name on a piece of paper stuck up by the bar. I did this one year, and I overheard someone say, 'He'll do anything for publicity.' This annoyed me because I've only ever behaved like a local in Hatch End. Nevertheless, it did make me think about how, because it's a pub, some people feel free to be openly critical of those in my profession, in a way that they would never be to those in any other. For example, if someone came up to a plumber in a pub and said, 'You're a bloody joke, mate,' they'd probably get a punch on the nose. However, it seems to be okay to say to someone who works on TV, 'I saw that crap you were in last night,' and not expect a reaction. I think it's partly to let you know that they're not impressed by you and I've never really been comfortable with that particular burden of celebrity.

Although Hatch End is genteel, with a lot of grey and white hair about, that doesn't mean to say that it's without its humour. Like any good pub, my current local is full of characters and occasionally you hear stories about people around here that bend you double with laughter. There was a story about Miss Barnett, an elderly lady who used to live on her own in a big house two doors down from us. She had a beloved pet dog called Bobby and every night, on the dot, she'd pop Bobby out for his bedtime pee. One night, later than usual, she let Bobby out, but when she called his name he didn't return. Miss Barnett grabbed a torch from her kitchen and walked down the road in search of Bobby, before finding him just a few yards away in flagrante with a bitch on heat. She shouted at him, and even went back home to fetch a bucket of water to throw on him, but nothing would put him off. Eventually, in desperation, she called her vet.

'It's Miss Barnett, of Hatch End,' she said.

'Hmmm.'

'My dog Bobby is at it with a bitch down the road.'

'Hmmm.'

'I've tried everything and I can't separate them. What should I do?'

Wearily, the vet replied, 'Bring him to the phone.'

'Will that stop him?' asked the old lady.

'I don't know,' said the vet, 'but it's just stopped me.'

When Ronnie Barker lived in Pinner, he just wanted to fit in. It was therefore a big surprise when I opened our local paper one day to read that Ronnie was to be the guest of honour at a fête in Harrow. 'My God,' I thought, 'that's a first. I have to see this.' Terry and I went along to see Ronnie sitting on a dais, signing autographs. So I found a screwed-up bit of paper, which I dirtied by rubbing it on the ground, turned my collar up and joined the queue. When it came to my turn I shoved the crumpled paper under his nose and in a comedy voice said, 'Would you put "to Margery", please?' He scribbled away but never looked up, and as I left, I felt that the joke had fallen rather flat.[2] Then I looked at the piece of paper.

'Piss off, Cryer,' it read, 'I'm busy.'

For Better or Worse[1]

Marriage is like paying an endless visit in your worst clothes.

J.B. PRIESTLEY

I consider myself incredibly fortunate to have met my wife Terry.[2] She'd been working in show business from the age of sixteen and, originally, ballet was her passion, but she was considered too tall to make it professionally. She retrained as a singer and won parts in West End musicals like *The Pajama Game*, *Carousel* and *Damned Yankees*. We have four children: Tony, a film lecturer, Dave, a web designer and family historian, Jack, a singer and choir conductor, and Bob, an actor and writer. Terry and I were never showbiz parents in the sense that we pushed them in the direction of entertainment and personally, I had no preconceived ideas of what they'd do in life. All that counted was that they were happy, and I'm very proud of them all.

We went to see Bob in a play at the West Yorkshire Playhouse in Leeds that was written by Steve Martin. It was called *Picasso at the Lapin Agile* and for some reason during

---

1 Terry keeps her counsel on this one.
2 For her side of the story, you can read her book *I Don't Get It: How to Survive Being Married to a Comedian* by Terry Cryer, Uxorious Books (1978).

its US run it never made it to Broadway. When *Steppenwolf* director Randall Arney and producer Thelma Holt decided to bring it to UK, Steve Martin agreed to come and see it. 'Steve Martin in conversation with Sir Ian McKellen', who was playing Lear at the theatre, was booked and for a few weeks there was a real buzz that these two amazing talents would be together on a stage in Leeds. Unfortunately, Steve was filming *Bowfinger* at the time and it overran, so he wasn't able to make it. It was a real shame, because the show was brilliant. Our son played Elvis and I remember him making a hell of an entrance, accompanied by spectacular backlighting and fireworks. He didn't sing, but everything he said came directly from the lyrics of Elvis songs. The local papers loved it, and I (perhaps biased) thought it was a wonderful show. However, I was cross when the national press, who had made the daring journey out of London to the wilds of Leeds to review it, were rather snide about it.

Rejection like this hurts and you never get one hundred per cent used to it, even if you're Steve Martin. It's hard not to take it personally but surviving it is just what you have to do. I still get scripts sent to me and these days, there's very little I can do with them but I usually write back and say, 'please don't take this to heart, just keep on writing and it will happen.' Rejection is, sadly, the name of the game. As a result, I've learnt not to dwell, which might appear insensitive sometimes but I try not to let the bad experiences linger. I might learn from them, but once I've had them, they quickly pass. If someone asks me whether or not I was upset by something bad that happened to me in the past, the honest answer will be that I can't remember how I felt at the time. Maybe it's a simplistic philosophy, but I think it's stood me in good stead.

Something I've never really understood is that good experiences can have the same effect on me as bad ones. If I've had a good show or someone's passed a compliment I get a warm glow for a minute and almost immediately it's gone. So later on, I find it hard to remember how happy I felt at the time. I wonder whether it's a Yorkshire thing, the feeling of reining yourself in because otherwise you might end up too big for your boots. When I worked as a stagehand at the Empire Theatre in Leeds I remember someone coming in one afternoon to tell us that Norman Wisdom would be playing at the theatre in the next few months. At that time, in the early 1950s, Norman was about as big as you get in Britain, and having him in Leeds was a real coup. One of the older stagehands took in the information, then said,

'If you can make them laugh here, you can make them laugh anywhere.'

I thought that summed up Yorkshire very well indeed. They are proud people who aren't easily impressed, and who, happy or sad, don't dwell on their feelings. I have an obsession with not getting too pleased with myself and I know it's something that lies deep within me. Terry complains that I can't take a compliment. If someone says they've enjoyed something I've done, I always say something like, 'oh, so you were the one!' 'Why do you always have to undercut it?' says Terry. 'Why can't you be more like that nice Mike Palin and just say "thanks"?' I have no answer to that, save to say that he's from Sheffield and they probably do things differently there.

The Empire Strikes Back

Therefore, it was with my usual mixture of embarrassment and pleasure that I got the OBE in 2001. I was unsure about the 'Empire' bit, not being much of a one for that sort of thing and I think it's time that the title of the award was changed to reflect the present day. However, I was more concerned about the fair amount of piss-taking I would receive from friends, which I duly received. I was also worried, too, that it had been bestowed on me from 'On High', but then I found out that your friends and peers have to nominate you for it. I felt much better than I might have done if it had been a Government sponsored gong. Many people have refused such honours, of course, and when I heard about mine I instantly recalled being with Eric Morecambe when he and Ernie got the news that they'd been given an OBE. Eric had always mocked awards and often took the mickey whenever someone he knew got a medal or was knighted. Eric went quiet about it for a few days, so one afternoon I thought I'd stir it up a little bit.

'I haven't heard much about you and your honour lately, Eric,' I said.

'Well,' he muttered, 'it would be rude to refuse.'

Despite being a little sceptical about the honour, I have to agree with Eric. I know it's a quaint custom, but someone, somewhere said, 'Oh, give the old boy a gong.' It's very nice to know that you're thought of in this way, even if you never find out who nominated you.[1]

When the day arrived, I went to Buckingham Palace and picked up the award from the Queen.[2] There were about a hundred of us there that morning, and before you step forward she's handed a bit of paper with something about you written on it.[3] I was impressed by the effort she put into it, and the way she had a little word with everyone, just to make it feel that bit personal. When it was my turn I went forward and she said, 'Are you still writing?' Well, I wasn't much, but I didn't think it was the time or place to get into that discussion[4] so I said that I was and she said, 'Keep it up.' My mind raced with a few responses to that comment, but it's a family show, so I'll move on.

If we're talking about honours, then I guess that I've ful-filled the showbiz clichés of appearing on both 'This Is Your Life' and 'Desert Island Discs'. The latter was during the short reign of Michael Parkinson on the show, before Sue Lawley took over. I was invited to a reunion of 1,000 'cast-aways' at the Reform Club in London. Bamber Gascoigne came over to speak to me. 'You did it during the Parky year,' he said, 'and so did I. We're the unfashionable ones here.'

I can blame Willie Rushton for 'This Is Your Life'. He rang me one day to tell me that he and I had been asked to take part in a pilot show about double acts, to be presented by Barry Took.

---

1 Jeffrey Archer, it's over to you. I know I said I'd settle for lunch, but . . .
2 Luckily, she was in.
3 Mine said 'Run'.
4 My agent thinks differently.

'I don't really want to do it, to be honest,' Will said. 'How about you?'

'Oh come on,' I said, ever keen to try something new. 'Why not? It might be fun, and besides, it's Tooky.'

'OK,' he said, 'I will if you will.'

Will had lured me in by getting me to persuade him to do it. It was a typically brilliant Rushton psychological trick and I fell for it straight away. The alarm bells didn't even ring when, a day or two later, I discovered a note by our home phone that read, 'This Is Your Life' with a number next to it in Terry's handwriting. I tackled her about it and she said,

'It was nothing. Besides,' she said enigmatically, 'it's not relevant any more.'

I thought no more about it and on the day of the pilot show a car came to pick me up. All the way to the studio, the driver kept answering a stream of calls by saying, 'We're on our way,' and I must confess that I thought a big deal was being made of me heading to a pilot show. Little did I know that following behind was another car with Terry and all the kids in it.

We arrived, and there was the studio, an audience, and Tooky, just as expected. Barry started talking about double acts and I was mentally rehearsing a few anecdotes when on walked a guy carrying a book. At first I thought it was the floor manager until I realised that the book was red and the guy was Michael Aspel.

The music started and I thought it was for Will, until I realised that he'd already been on the show. Then, Michael came over and said, 'Barry.' Even at this stage, I thought it must be Tooky. Suddenly, the curtain went up and there was the 'This Is Your Life' set. I was ushered into the chair and Terry and the kids joined me. Of course, she was a prime mover behind the organisation of the show and she'd compiled a fantastic list of people she thought I'd like to see.⁵ Most of my friends were on and when Humph appeared with his trumpet and played 'We'll Meet Again' with Colin Sell at the piano, I could've died and gone to heaven.⁶

'This Is Your Life' was a great experience but it wasn't asked for and if it hadn't happened I wouldn't have been any different. I was on a high afterwards, but as usual, it didn't last long. Besides, I had to work the following day. I'm lucky that I've got the family to keep me busy and I hope this means I maintain an offstage life. Many people I worked with wore their public persona all day long, and that can't have been easy at all. Still, I like working, and while I'm happy to read, go to the theatre or cinema or go for a drink in the local with my mates, I'm always very happy when a bit of work is thrown into the mix. I can go without writing or working in general for a while, but after that I become itchy and need a challenge.

Retiring or, as it so often happens in this business, being retired by the lack of phone calls, wouldn't sit very easily with me. I think I'd hate it. Ronnie Barker opened an antiques shop after retiring but I just can't walk away from it.

---

5 She'd included a fair few women but Thames Television had decided to create an almost all-male guest list. Only one woman, Brenda Bear, with whom I was at university, appeared. I was a bit disappointed by that.
6 Maybe it was the nightclub this time, I can't recall.

To Split Infinitives and Beyond

I acted in a film quite recently, directed by the writer Peter Vincent, who's an old colleague of mine. He wanted me to play a vicar, which I was happy to do. I tried out the vicar in my own voice at first. It didn't really work, so Peter suggested something just a touch more actorly and, trying hard not to overdo it, I came up with a kind of Barry Cryer/Alec Guinness hybrid. As usual, though, I didn't get round to learning my lines. I spent most of the day apologising, so they kindly wrote them out for me in big print. I really enjoyed it but I felt slightly like Tony Hancock, staring into the distance at a cue card. I suppose it catches up with us all but I didn't enjoy that particular kind of senior moment.

I have mentioned Alan Bennett quite a few times throughout this book and it's still one of my ambitions to be in something written by him. The thought of learning lines and doing eight shows a week brings me out in a cold sweat, but if it was an Alan Bennett play, I think I could bear it. Terry and I went to see the revival of *Enjoy* recently and I was reminded of his incredible use of language. He knows just when to place words, so they arrive immaculately on the ear. I spoke to him earlier this year, during the heavy snowfall in London, and we talked about the right footwear for the weather. 'Oh,' he said, 'we've haven't anything *approaching* a Wellington here.' Approaching. That's Alan – a class act.

I've also become a big fan of Ricky Gervais. I think he's an exceptional talent. I love the way he sends up the phoniness and ridiculousness of celebrity and yet appears to be impressed by the calibre of guests he has on 'Extras'. He's ridiculing the whole daft thing, but getting a buzz from it at the same time. That interests me. A few years ago I was on my annual visit to the Groucho Club and there were Ricky Gervais and Steve Merchant. Steve I'd met because he was at university with my son, Bob, but I wasn't sure that I'd met Ricky.

'Don't you remember being in a studio in a cellar in Soho a few years ago doing a pilot of a show that never happened. In it was this pretty young man. That was me!'

I'd like to call that a senior moment too, but unfortunately I've got form. I did the same to the writer John Sullivan. I was watching 'Only Fools and Horses' one night and I was so impressed by the particular episode that I rang him to say that I thought it was terrific. He thanked me, then I said,

'We've never met?'

There was a terrible pause.

'What do you mean?' he said. 'I started off as a stagehand working on 'The Two Ronnies' and I used to put the occasional joke in, which was accepted. Me and the rest of the stagehands were in the BBC bar once, all of us looking at the great men – Cryer, Vosburgh and Nobbs. Then you came over and said "hello".'

I can at least take comfort in that.

Afterword

I hope you have enjoyed reading this book. Watch out for the sequel: *Harry Potter and the Da Vinci Code.*[1] My thanks to the Inland Revenue, who have been a tower of strength in compelling me to write this book.

So, if today has been a good one, enjoy that, and if it hasn't then look forward to tomorrow. I have several mottos – one is ABC: Always Be Cooperative, Avoid Being Compromised. I've always gone with the flow, and somehow I've meandered my way around a life that I wouldn't change a second of. The bad parts as well as the good.

I almost gave this business up when I was young, because I suffered terribly from eczema. Having to wear lots of heavy stage make-up, like you did in those days, played hell with it and I thought it wasn't for me. Perhaps I was already considering writing instead of performing, I don't know. However, as I was trying to work it all out, I met Terry and I only went into hospital once more for treatment after that. I never had an occurrence of it again. I don't think it's a coincidence that it cleared up just after I met her. I still think I'm an itchy character, always keen for something new to come along, but I'm grateful that it's now under the skin, not on top of it.

---

1 In which Soames and Irene discover the Ark of the Covenant and defeat the Nazis in the Egyptian desert.

My wife and I went to a show in Poole, Dorset, and the woman tearing the tickets mistook me for Michael Palin. I've never had that one before, so I rang him the next day and told him, and he said, 'So it's your turn.' The most unlikely people get mistaken for each other. Take Roy Hudd,[2] for years people have said to him, 'Where's the emu?' Personally, I've got quite a gallery. Barry Took obviously features very strongly, because of the white hair and glasses. I went into the local newsagents a while ago and the woman behind the counter said, 'Oh Dorothy look who's here ... I never miss "The Goodies".' 'Neither do I,' I riposted. I never found out which one they meant.[3]

Oliver Postgate, the master of children's TV puppetry, who created Bagpuss and the Clangers, once defined himself as 'a verb, not a noun'. 'If I'm not doing something,' he said, 'I don't exist.'

Well, I've enjoyed being a verb and I hope never to be a noun.

Barry Cryer,
Dunquippin' Rest Home
Haddam-against-the-Wall
Herts
July 2009

PS 'A book may be amusing, with numerous errors, or it may be very dull without a single absurdity.' – Oliver Goldsmith. Count my numerous errors and I hope you spot the odd absurdity.

---

2 But I want him back.
3 Dorothy. Make that call.

PPS 'The moving finger writes and, having writ, moves on.' Edward FitzGerald.[4]

PPPS Hold on. Newsflash: Well-loved, popular comedian and writer Barry Cryer died yesterday when a beer barrel fell on his head. It took a day to remove the barrel and two weeks to wipe the smile off his face.

---

[4] See you same time tomorrow.

Index

Reviews

'Once I put it down, I couldn't pick it up.'   Jonathan Ross

'Exhilarating, elevating, uplifting, transporting and intoxicating.'   Peter Roget

'Revealing and yet in an indefinable way, strangely opaque, although quintessentially translucent.'   Wayne Rooney

'A complete waste of time.'   Stephen Hawking

John Treham -